Kathle

Inside-Out

Inside-Out:
Stories and Methods for Generating Collective Will to Create the Future We Want

By
Tracy Huston

society for SOL organizational learning

Published by SoL, The Society for Organizational Learning, Inc.
25 First Street, Suite 414
Cambridge, MA 02141 USA
1-617-300-9500
publisher@solonline.org

SoL is a nonprofit global membership organization that connects researchers,
organizations, and consultants to create and implement knowledge for
fundamental learning and change. A portion of the net proceeds from SoL
publishing sales are reinvested in basic research, leading-edge applied learning
projects, and building a global network of learning communities. For
information on projects, membership, professional development opportunities,
events, or other publications—including the e-journal *Reflections*—please visit
www.solonline.org.

Book design: Frank Ladd

Library of Congress Control Number: 2007925254

ISBN 10: 0-9742390-6-2

Dedicated to my children,
Grace and Max,
and to the many inspired leaders
in our businesses and communities
who are engaged in healing our societies and planet —
for the future of all our children

Contents

Prologue to the Source of Change

   i.   The Price   1

   ii.   Enough   5

   iii.   The Movement   8

   iv.   The Holding Space   15

   v.   The Well(ness)   20

   vi.   Little Things with Profound Effects   22

The Way In

   Putting the People Back in Purpose   27

   New Forms to Follow New Functions   29

   The View from the Middle of the Mess   37

   The Starting Point: Inside-Out   42

   Collective Interiors   48

   The No-Excuse Clause   57

   Staying True   61

Act One: Ensemble Approaches to Working from the Inside-Out

   Overture: Many Instruments, Playing a Shared Song   65

Ensemble Work   66

From Crisis to Chaos   67

Ensemble Improvisation as a Means to Innovation and Adaptability   69

Requisite Competencies for Ensemble Improvisation   74

Ensemble Improvisation Methods   77

De-mechanization Methods: Freeing the Body to Perceive   80

    Physical Meditation   84

    Walking Conscious   87

    Working in Slow-Reverse   88

    Bubbling Up   90

Situation: Observation and Perception Methods — Connecting to Collective Interiors   93

    No-Man's Land   95

    Pure Observation   97

    Shared Reality   102

    Story Weaving   106

    One Story, Many Voices and Movements   113

Intention and Will Methods: Connecting the Source to the Situation   120

    Shared Will and Role Creation   121

Ensemble Performance Methods: Putting the Shared Story on Its Feet   127

    Interactive Theatre   128

Summary of Methods   131

Act Two: One Square Mile — Building the Future We Want, One Block at a Time

Building from the Inside-Out, Ground-Up   138

    One Square Mile   139

The Way Forward
  Menlo Lab   147
  The Menlo Lab Approach   148
  Invitation   150

Acknowledgements   153
References and Sources   155

Prologue to
the Source of Change

i. The Price

I had been working with senior executives from around the world for several years, noticing what was a once subtle and only vaguely defined expression of despair, (uttered only in the privacy of coaching sessions or conversations otherwise protected by virtue of friendship), suddenly mushroom into a deafening collective and highly public uproar: [the human price we are paying to struggle to survive if not thrive in the new global economy, awash in uncertainty about both the forces at play and our roles as leaders in it, has far exceeded the value any one of us are deriving from it.] Group after group of executives began to cry out, each time more adamantly, confessing at once to be victims of burnout under extreme pressure to eke out just a bit more profit under increasingly difficult circumstances and at the same time themselves the oppressors who were necessarily squeezing out every drop of productivity their dwindling headcounts could muster. In one working session, the executives drew a horrifying picture of what their world looked like, illustrated as a man-eating machine gobbling up employees to feed its insatiable hunger for profit, the controls of the machine manned by an evil puppet king dangling his executive committee on marionette strings, forcing them to

feed more and more employees into the jaws of the machine, fuel for the enterprise to burn. During another session, a leadership team suggested that one of the company core values might be "happiness", and the group gazed on the word in thoughtful silence, as if it were a long-forgotten but beautiful dream; but then they sadly shook their heads and drew a line through the word on the flip chart, for we had taught them to keep only those values they thought the company would live by. The same group suggested that the central role of leadership should be restoring "Quality of Life" throughout the enterprise, but couldn't come to any conclusions about how to do it and still make their numbers.

In more sessions than I can count, the work was followed by long nights of drinking themselves into collective oblivion, where men (most of them men) would suddenly turn to me, eyes streaming tears, to lament they returned home one night to see their children had grown up, but they had been so busy working that they hadn't even noticed. A friend who's an executive of an advanced technology engineering group told me that he woke up one day, and seeing his young daughter, was gripped by a panic and a renewed aspiration to develop that which would ensure her and the rest of the planet a healthy world, only to show up at work three months later to see his green technology program cut due to expense. Who has the money and the resources to think about sustainability, he asked, when we are barely now surviving? Who has time to even *think?*

Colleagues who work with other companies express the same alarming observations. It seems as if global business is on the brink of self-destruction. I have noticed the same pressures and same human prices being paid in school systems, healthcare, and government and nongovernmental agencies as well. The problems keep getting bigger and more complex, and so we keep feeding more of ourselves into them to fix them. We dump tons of money into new technologies to help, we create evermore sophisticated processes and systems to help (with the help of evermore sophisticated and expensive consulting resources), and yet even the

most valiant and well-planned change efforts fail to meet the challenges at hand, at least not for long. When we've exhausted the options our dwindling budgets afford, we go back to the only thing left, our "social capital", as if it were of unlimited supply. One executive likened this phenomenon to a hamster wheel—we run and run and run, only to find we haven't moved from the same old place!

Humans are the only living creatures that willingly impose such hardships on themselves; it is both unnatural and unnecessary to pay so great a **human price** for economic survival and general well-being. And yet, we continue to pay it as if we had no other recourse. *Why?*

FABLE

Man-in-the-Bush

Far, far away, in the middle of a sprawling city, there is a beautiful Japanese garden. The garden is tucked away between the right angles of towering hotels and office buildings, captive of streets and concrete. It would be easier for the garden to grow in the country, yet its cherry trees bloom each spring, its bamboo sprouts new shoots, the evergreens grow green the year long, each according to its own nature, not mindful of the city and its strange forms (tolerating the gardeners, as long as they don't interfere too much).

Walking home from dinner one night with some colleagues, after a long session with a group of executives, we followed the garden path home. The narrow path wound through a beautifully sculpted hillside of bamboo and fir, azalea in bloom, and over a little stream, the stepping stones of the path clinging still to the side of the hill, softly resolute, well worn by many travelers who had passed this way before.

Some ways down the path, a man approached. He

*was weaving precariously on the narrow path, stagger-
ing in his drunkenness. His tie was loosened, his jacket
disheveled, both of expensive make, the uniform of the
successful executive, now in disarray—an altogether
unnatural state for a person in a position such as he. As
he weaved his way toward us, I could see that his eyes
were half closed over a wildly broad grin that stretched
across his face, and that his cheeks were streaked with
tears. His body jerked with drunken spasms as he
walked, alien even in his own skin; yet on he trod as if
the grinning face alone would be enough to pull his
heavy weight along. He was a sorry sight, a freak of
nature in the garden.*

*Suddenly, the man stopped on the path, and
turned to face down the hillside. A large evergreen
bush lay at his feet, and he dropped his head to gaze at
it, as if he had never seen such a thing before. And
then, much to our surprise, the man bent stiffly at the
waist, and, almost in slow motion, as if performing a
dance or ancient ritual, followed his head straight into
the bush. He did not appear to fall, but rather to sub-
merge himself, an act that seemed quite intentional, as
if he could somehow shed his human form and instead
become branch and leaf, of earth and nature once
again. He landed right in the middle of the bush, his
head and upper torso completely immersed inside it,
with his feet firmly planted on the path outside it. And
then he stayed there, head in the bush, and did not
move. Of course, the bush rejected the man, as did the
earth beneath. But the man seemed intent, and waited,
head in the bush, his buttocks protruding into the air
like a signpost: how foolish is the world of men.*

*Afraid he might be injured, I ran to his aid. I called
once to ask if I might help, but he did not reply.
Uncertain whether or not he wanted to come out of the*

bush, I finally took his arm and slowly pulled him up.
He thanked me politely, both grinning and crying as
before, then tottered on down the path into the dark to
catch the last train home and a few hours of sleep
before he'd rise to do it all again.

The breeze chased after the man, sending the flow-
ers and leaves shivering, as if they, too, did not know
whether to laugh or to cry at the strange creatures that
are humans.

This fable is based on a true story. The company for which the
man-in-the-bush works has since hired a psychologist to help
them deal with the alarming rate of depression, alcoholism, and
related illness they are now encountering. This same company saw
record sales that year. But its executives are plainly saying that the
current practices that delivered those results are not sustainable.
No one's listening.

ii. Enough

On the night I started writing this little book, my fifteen
year-old daughter, Grace, and I were washing dishes, discussing
what she had been learning and thinking about in her American
History class, a series of conversations we had been having for
some time, loosely following the class syllabus from the second
World War, through the Korean War, Viet Nam, and, that night,
the Cuban Missile Crisis, these points in time interrupted by the
ongoing story of the invasion of Iraq by our own country, the
United States. The trajectory of these lessons painted a picture for
Grace of sure destruction of the human race, at the hands of the
human race (most likely the Americans). Through each conversa-

tion I could see her disgust, and either sensed or imagined the implied expectation that I and all the rest of the adults who had created these histories (even only if by allowing them to unfold and repeat), at the least, if we grownups could not behave better, should feel a reasonable amount of shame. But she would neither accuse nor condemn; she had come to the place I had most feared for her, a simple acceptance of the brutal facts, the sum of which (I had to admit) could not be whittled away by what was scarce evidence of change.

I remembered having the same feeling when I was Grace's age, then in the midst of the Cold War, the anger and constancy of a picture of the imminent end of humanity, each night filled with nightmares of the countless scenarios for mutually assured destruction (as furnished and described in minute detail by the US Department of Defense, simulated with painstaking accuracy in my own dream imagination), and how I was always surprised each morning when I woke up that we were, somehow, all still there. And then, on this night of washing dishes with my daughter, again that same surprise. I realized that too many dinners and dish washings had been consumed with talk of suicide bombs and war, massacres and starvation, AIDS and other impending plagues, climate change and the destruction of our planet. And I saw her world, a tenth grader in a school of 3500 in Los Angeles, where so many kids have only one parent who typically works two jobs, where more students are somehow affiliated with gangs than not (whether or not they actively participate as such), and where the vast majority are doing drugs (old ones and new ones whose names are unfamiliar to me), and in the daily midst of racial strife that sometimes erupts in riots and the occasional shooting, where her lost friends appear at our door having no other safe place to stay, no money in their pockets, no food to eat, no clean clothes to wear, the sons and daughters of addicts and the mentally ill or otherwise unfit, the physically and spiritually wounded that Grace collects as if she and she alone could shelter and nurse it all away—and all the teachers who try and the preachers and rabbis

and social workers and neighbors and friends who try, and somehow, each day, it is never enough. And as we stood there washing dishes, scrubbing, wiping, sweeping in an act of mutual comfort, I saw her insistence on facing this fact of the whole of her world, she recognizing herself lucky in the middle of it, and her stubborn love of it and the people in it, and yet, at the same time, her complete acceptance that it would never, ever change, not much anyway. We, the adults, had made a mess, a horrible, wretched mess, and, as far as she could tell, would continue doing so, such that, despite the good intentions and good work of a few, there were not enough people engaged in trying to make things right to save humanity, indeed, all things living, at least not enough to make a difference before our time was up.

She stated her perceptions quite matter-of-factly, without emotion or apparent fear or remorse. Despite my insistence that, while the extent of the mess could not be denied, there was now something changing, a new energy that was arising all over the world, growing fast and wide, drawing in more and more people who were determined to fix the mess, Grace held fast to her views, framing her final argument thus: we make people suffer unnecessarily, and have always done, and will always continue to do, and so the only way to end the suffering is to let humanity end itself. And while this did not mean she would not try to help change the miserable state of affairs, she did not think enough people would stand and up and act to make a real difference, at least not in time.

Her cool acceptance of this view stopped my heart, long enough that the world seemed for a moment to stop its spinning, life to cease its breathing.

But then, suddenly, there in the stillness, something unexpected happened: a lightness bubbled up through us, between us and around us, like a "**crack**" in a field of black that suddenly opened, a gateway to pass through, completely unobstructed, and in this gateway a better future that was already there, evident if only sensed, but quite as possible as anything else, almost ridiculously simple, reached as easy and natural as the river finds the sea.

And I felt: how little, how small a movement into this other place can be *enough*.

QUOTE

Leonard Cohen, *poet, musician*

Ring the bell that still can ring
Forget your perfect offering
There is a crack in everything
That's how the light gets in

iii. The Movement

When confronted with the complexity, magnitude, and, in many cases the horror of current reality, many of us feel a mighty movement of a kind never before enacted would be required to make real change—that the magnitude of the response must be equal to the magnitude of the challenge. Our habit is to thus create big institutions—governments, businesses, agencies—that by virtue of the volume of their resources and sophistication of their policies, processes, technologies, and systems might somehow be up to the challenge. But, as we can easily observe, bigger messes aren't being solved by bigger efforts. In fact, profound transformation of the kind that allows individuals and groups to perform extraordinary acts seems to arise from an invisible space, often *outside* of the prevailing structures and systems. For example, we can observe how ordinary people often perform heroic acts in the wake of natural disaster, in conditions where the familiar systems suddenly no longer exist.

Many have observed that profound individual and collective transformation most often occurs in response to crisis or great tragedy. Somehow these catastrophic events cause us to draw

from a source we otherwise ignore. This source seems to suddenly shift us into new ways of being that can transcend even the most complex social, economic, and political obstacles. Recently, large-scale **collective transformation** of this kind occurred quite unexpectedly at my daughter's high school, when a student, a friend of Grace's, was shot and killed. Somehow, the tragedy of this student's death caused the entire student body of 3500 to transcend their differences and instantaneously shift themselves into new ways of being with each other. Here is the story of what happened:

(living) EXAMPLE

In Memory of Eddie Lopez

Eddie Lopez was only fifteen when he was shot, shot dead. The day after it happened, the kids showed up at school wearing t-shirts with Eddie's picture printed on them, over the letters R.I.P. (Rest In Peace). The t-shirt design had been carefully crafted in insistence on peace, obstruction of rage and any desire for revenge, for it was unanimously held that Eddie's death was unjust, more unjust than most, because he had lived as most could not—Eddie Lopez was the son of immigrants from Mexico, the first in his family who would go to college, straight-A student, and star of the high school baseball team. He was loved by everyone, blacks and whites, Asians and Persians and Latinos, a phenomenon that was noticed even before his death because it was so rare; kids of different colors don't mix, at least not much. It's a big city school, racial tensions the norm. There had even been a riot that broke out between the blacks and the Latinos earlier in the year. But everybody loved Eddie, and the fact that it was him now dead made it somehow more intolerable than death usually is.

The news had spread fast the night he was killed;

cell phones and AIM. At first, everybody wanted to know what had happened. Rumors were that he'd been shot on Pico by some kid in the Sawtelle gang. That didn't make sense; Eddie wasn't in a gang; he'd stead-fastly refused the lure of the gangs, the pressure to join. Then it got around that the shooting was a drive-by; that made more sense, people are always getting shot up in drive-bys, often innocent bystanders, old ladies and little kids, people who don't notice the gangster car turning a corner, idling slow up the street, and just happen to walk blindly into a bullet heading another direction, wrong place at the wrong time. It was then speculated: they didn't mean to kill Eddie; it was sure-ly an accident, the drive-by intended to hit another boy instead, Eddie's friend, one of two boys who had been walking up the street with him when it happened. The new realization changed the tone of the conversation, and rumors quickly spread: Eddie's friend had just dumped his girlfriend, who was known to be the sister of a boy in the Sawtelle gang; people surmised she called the hit. By midnight there was consensus: it was definitely an accident, Eddie the unintended victim, his death the jilted girlfriend's fault, and her vengeance-hungry brother the shooter.

At some point an eyewitness emerged, identity undisclosed. Just where this witness was when the shooting occurred was unclear (later, a troubling point, as the death might have been avoided had the witness acted rather than paused). Anyway, somehow it got around that Eddie's friends ran when they heard the shots; who wouldn't. But people started to get angry when the wonder spread: why did they leave him, why didn't they go back when the gangsters' car was gone? Eddie wouldn't have left his friends to die like that. But Eddie was hit so bad he couldn't even walk, dragged

himself up the sidewalk over a whole city block trying to find help, leaving a swath of blood behind. More and more questions spread over wires and wireless: Pico Boulevard is busy, so why did it take so long before someone called an ambulance? Who called the ambulance? Didn't Eddie have a cell phone? Didn't his friends? Where did he die? Why did he have to die?

Despite the simmering anger that had bubbled through the night, by morning, somehow the entire student body had generated the collective act of will to defy the impulse for retaliation. The frozen images of Eddie's face were worn and walked about in deliberate, controlled defiance throughout the campus, a painstakingly calculated move on the part of the kids so as to structure attention on the boy and not the acts and facts surrounding his death. No one, not even the gangs, would disrupt what needed to be done. Immediate and coordinated action was required, and a discipline for such: they needed to organize a memorial service, and the family needed money so they could get their son's body out of the hospital morgue, pay for a funeral and a white hearse where the boy would be sealed away safe in a box, which, his family and friends would pray, would be delivered to heaven, where the archangel Michael would be sure to let him in, because Eddie was a good boy, one of the best; if you're good in this life, you get in, that's the rule, and Eddie was especially good in light of the bad odds to which he'd been born in, in consideration of the fact he'd refused to join a gang even when his friends did, even when just about everyone did, and everybody loved him just the same, even people from the same gang who shot him dead. Maybe that doesn't amount to much in your view. But, you must understand that here you're more likely to be in a gang than not. When you're in a gang, you got peo-

ple who'll watch your back, help you take care of business. You got a family. Everybody knows it's messed up, but for a lot of people it's not like there's alternatives. But Eddie wasn't, wouldn't, and that meant something to the rest of the kids, even gang kids, especially them.

So when the students self-organized a memorial service at school the day after Eddie was shot, more kids showed up in the campus' Greek Theatre than you get in a homecoming pep rally, about 3500 of them: Latinos, blacks, whites, Asians, Persians; everybody came. All the gangs were represented: Shoreline, V13, Sawtelle, Bloods, Crips, and the newer Persian gang from east of Sepulveda. People cried who'd never cried before, at least not in public. Strangers, friends, and enemies held each other. The school symphony played, some kids rapped, and others made speeches, the choir sang, all impromptu, loosely arranged the night before via wired and wireless will. Miraculously, instead of rage, there was love.

How did that happen? Grace said that Eddie made a space, like a circle, that somehow everybody wanted to gather up inside.

Heaven ... heaven is a place ... a place where nothing ... nothing ever happens— [1]

After the funeral was over, whatever "space" Eddie had created was buried with him. Grace says the kids are even more cynical than before—it's messed up when you stay out of gangs, try to live right, and get shot dead anyway. Some of the gang kids said he would've been better off had he joined, so they would've been watching his back. Others said the odds are just as good you get shot anyway, doing gang business, watching other peoples' backs for them. Others

said it's human nature, everybody wants to be on top, thinking for themselves, just like the US, George Bush and the rest of them.

But the space for love and peace was there, for a whole long week.

Where did it go?

How can we get it back again?

It's always there, this invisible power within us—it appears suddenly, often unexpectedly, and then retreats again. But it's there. We've all experienced times of crisis when we and others have tapped into this source to do and be in ways we never thought possible. What's more, this source somehow allows us to take significant collective action in the *absence* of any structure, authority, rules and preordained roles. There was no "big thing" out there to structure the action the kids in my daughter's school took to organize Eddie's memorial service. They had no process map to follow, the teachers did not lead it or suggest it, and the externally imposed rules for getting along which had previously failed to maintain peace across ethnic divides were replaced with an invisible, unspoken rule that allowed them to transcend their differences. In these types of events, it is not the external forms of power, organization, and process that guide, but rather an ***invisible yet powerful force*** that comes from inside us.

SCIENCE

String Theory & Brane Worlds

Scientists have recently discovered this invisible power as well: the universe, they now say, sprang from an infinitely small speck of space-time known as a singularity, a contradiction in the laws of nature which hold that nothing can be infinitely small. How can something as infinitely big as the universe arise from this

infinitely small space?

For some time now, scientists have been troubled by the fact that 90% of matter that should be here is missing. All the "pieces" that should be needed to create the reality we see and feel are not here; in fact, all we have are mere projections, like shadows cast from pieces in other realms. In a recent scientific breakthrough, physicist Joe Polchinski tracked the missing matter—we were looking in the wrong place. According to Joe, we are stuck on a thin membrane ("brane" for short), a boundary like the surface of a pond where the water meets the sky, but which can know neither the sky above nor what lurks in the water below. Our brane separates us from the rest of the cosmos, a vast "bulk" comprised of countless branes in other dimensions, some of which may contain the missing matter (or other scientists looking for their missing pieces). Branes are a place where things (matter) become stuck, like scum floating on the surface of a pond. While matter sticks to our brane, gravity leaks. (For some reason, gravity tends to be very weak.) The curious thing is that matter depends on gravity to keep it all together, yet gravity is leaking in greater proportions than needed for matter to take form. Luckily, according to String Theory, matter is not made up of tiny, point-like particles, but rather "strings" that vibrate in as many as ten dimensions; Joe figures there must be enough matter on hidden branes in other dimensions with enough mass to generate enough gravity to keep us altogether. It is, somehow, enough.

(**Source:** LA Times article, May 17, 2003)

This source is always within us. It is both immense and invis-

ible, elusive and ever-present. It appears as a sudden movement from the old self, the old complex set of relationships and habits and acts, and springs suddenly into a new way of being that can overcome what was previously deemed insurmountable. Thought leaders such as Otto Scharmer have suggested that we turn our attention to this source, a movement he calls "presencing".[2] Scharmer likens this shift to the work of an artist: the attention moves from the result, the finished *painting*, even from process, the *act of painting*, to the source, the *blank canvas*. This is what we are confronted with in crisis, when all the familiar structures, rules and roles no longer exist. How, he asks, can we learn to live from this blank canvas as a natural state of being?

How can we learn to draw from this source to proactively, positively effect profound change? How can we intentionally create such a movement that allows us to shed the old stuck self and ways of being and thus emerge into a new state of co-existence?

The work of many, now gathering in so many places, is something about holding open this space, this invisible singularity that is there in any one of us as much as all of us, this center and this source of us that is enough.

This little book is about holding this space, for Grace, for Eddie, for myself, and others who are doing the work of transforming the habit of making messes into the will to create the future we want.

iv. The Holding Space

The night of washing dishes with my daughter occurred just after I had returned from a gathering of some two dozen people from all over the world, members of the Presencing Institute[3] that MIT professor and author Otto Scharmer had convened in order to explore ways to tap into this invisible but powerful source so as

to generate profound and sustainable change. The gathering
included leaders from great institutions ranging from the United
Nations and European Union, MIT and the University of
Amsterdam, Oxfam and local grassroots education and AIDS projects, even from big business (such as myself). We came from
countries as disparate as South Africa and France, India and
Australia, New Zealand and Guatemala, Germany and the United
States, having been drawn to each other through a shared sense
that this source, this "singularity of movement", could be tapped
and embodied to effect profound and sustainable change. Among
us was a preacher who had moved his work from the pulpit to the
street in order to help people caught in messes, those in need, like
prostitutes and drug addicts, gangs, and criminals, and who has
since become the unofficial mayor of the refugees from Hurricane
Katrina who were flown without choice across the country from
New Orleans to a camp on Cape Cod. Also in this group were
those on the front lines of the AIDS epidemic, of the schools
where kids kill each other over offences as seemingly small as an
accidental bump in a hallway or stepping on the toe of a gangster's
shoe, and those who battle the vile networks that specialize in the
global trafficking of women, now reported in dollars to be the fifth
largest global industry. In reflecting on my conversation with my
daughter, and the fact of this group of people, I can say: yes, we
have a made a mess, a whole bunch of messes, but, no, it is not for
lack of people who have dedicated their lives to cleaning them up
that they persist. There are tons of people engaged in dealing with
The Mess. It is just that the messes are so deep and so wide that
all these good people have barely any space left for themselves,
much less to start fresh, to build another future. How can such
people have space for anything but for managing the messes at
hand? Yet they observe they must have space as well for the
future. How then, this group of leaders has asked, can we create
space for both dealing with the messes *and* for surfacing another
way of *being*, one that stops producing all of these messes? And,
more, how can we turn our attention away from things like mess-

es (the exterior), to the source, the interior condition of the **self** as an actor in the world, and to the **collective** who share one world, one source, one story that is, in fact, of our own creation?

METAPHOR

Tuning the Self to Play a Shared Song

It is said that the self is like a musical instrument, through which the song, the infinite potential of humanity, emerges. Our experience of life might be likened to a musical improvisation, in which each note we play builds on the last, our past, and comes from a place in the future, from any number of notes we might play to explore the song.

Sometimes it feels easier to replay only the notes we know, to repeat the same thoughts, deeds, ways of being over and over again; when this happens, the potential of the song, our life, becomes limited, stuck in repeating loops in the same time and space, keeping new movements, new ways of being, from emerging. The term "presencing" refers in large part to the work we do in tuning the instrument, the self, to allow us to move from repeating patterns (notes) of the past, and to let come the full potential of what we might bring into our songs from the larger field of the future—the vast potential we have yet to grasp and bring into being, present but as yet only sensed.

This work on the self seems critical, the central challenge of leadership. Yet to imagine that each of us has only our own song to play is likely an illusion. Transforming the power of each individual instrument into collective action requires us, somehow, to play a shared song. The "holding space" is a container that can help the many voices to "presence" the shared song we wish to play together.

The Presencing Institute, just forming at the time of this writing, has set out to explore ways to create a "holding space", the time and place and people and practices, strong enough to deal with both the current realities and co-creation of a better future. This group is intended to function as an action research network, a living lab, that could effect profound transformation across the many dimensions of our global and local systems—the web of relationships that sustain our lives through education and healthcare, government and business, environment and economies, societies and the local communities which reflect the whole. Briefly summarized, the work of this institute centers on creating "living examples" that represent each facet of this huge, complex system, and to nurture these examples through:

1) research about what can make them work better, independently and collectively;

2) the development of new social technologies (concrete methods and practices) that might help us draw from this deep source within us to transform ourselves and, thus, the systems we lead and participate within;

3) the discipline of capacity building to enable us to act from a deeper place within the self in service of the collective, and thus, to act in harmony with a larger field of change;

4) the development of what is called a "social presencing theatre," a way to mirror current realities and reflect back to society new futures that are emerging, and how these arise.

As a starting point, the "living examples" that could be nurtured in this holding space range from HIV/AIDS programs in South Africa and Washington D.C. to sustainable food projects in Australasia, global green technology projects transforming the automotive industry to education programs in Fitchburg, Massachusetts improving the futures of Latino children in the

community—and more. Any of these projects is in itself extremely complex, with challenges that have long gone unresolved or have deepened, despite the tremendous dedication and self-sacrifice of the people tackling them. Adding the dimension of interrelationship among all the projects as parts of an intertwined system is even more overwhelming. Yet this is precisely the nature of the challenge to be addressed, to deal with *wholes* rather than continually trying to fix the many broken parts in isolation.

As physically, emotionally, and spiritually stretched as the leaders of these living examples might be, throughout the two-day meeting, we heard ourselves and our co-participants saying that, while everything appears to be crumbling in the world, a new energy, a new movement was clearly emerging, and we were ready to go with it. At the same time, a phrase kept surfacing: "we don't have much time". The group energy was very high, acute in its focus and somehow loving in its embrace of the magnitude of the problems and each other in creating such a space to hold them all together. But again and again the phrase kept coming back: we don't have much time. I noticed the way in which the phrase was spoken, and wondered at it, for it was stated from a place of apparent peace, or an acceptance similar to the way my daughter had articulated it. In me it raised a fear, almost a deep dread. I kept listening harder to the others who repeated it, trying to sense and see what they could see that might keep my nightmares at bay. But while I was worrying, something was happening, in me and in the group: a space had indeed started to emerge that could hold both the end and a new beginning. (A "space" such as I mean to describe is a funny thing, for it is invisible yet palpable. It appears from inner knowing and clear intention, and a very deep will. And while it is not necessarily observable or measurable, not knowable in our rational way of knowing, it has a volume and an energy that is enough to change our ways of seeing—indeed, what we actually perceive—and, consequently, the quality of our actions in ways far beyond what ordinary efforts and initiatives can yield.) And so we set about exploring ways to hold this space, how to enlarge it,

how to allow our intentions and our actions to emerge through it, so that, at last, a different future might emerge. We agreed to continue this exploration and the work of enacting what we learn and learning from what we enact, through our "living examples". The work would help us as leaders to develop our own "instruments", as well as the emerging "song".

Over the course of our two days together, and hearing reports of many other groups like ours, now flourishing throughout the world, I am relieved to report that the grownups my daughter and myself as a child had been looking for have appeared. And they are not going away. Like a mother cradling a child, they and countless others like them are making a space that can hold humanity together.

v. The Well(ness)

The nature of this holding space is emergent—present and appearing, sustaining and expanding. It is, to me, like a well, described by some as "collective wisdom"[4] that both transcends self and arises from it. What is this well, this source, and why do we not easily draw from it? Here is a little fable that describes my *hypothesis*:

FABLE

The Well

We are a forest of trees clinging to the side of a steep mountain.
We forgot that we started from tiny seeds
That had to learn to grow,
To sense how and what it is, growing,
Whose only guide was a well

Deep within the earth, a vast, invisible pool
That held both the source of nourishment and way of
being
Of all the trees that had come before and would yet be.

Photo by Megumi Isard-Kuroda

And so, at first we drank deeply from the well, for we
knew of nothing else.
And we drank and drank until we grew all the way as
high as we could be.
And, once at our height, grown up,
We felt somehow finished with our growing,
And thus took to sustaining our selves, grown, what it
was that we had come to be,
As we were, finished
Living off rain
No longer in need of the well that is for growing
Living off wind
Bending slightly this way and that to catch a bit more
sun, a little more shade
Thinking this was enough.

When a fire comes and consumes the forest,
Leaving only our roots underneath the surface,
Rain is not enough, wind is not enough, nor sun
To start again
And so, the roots go searching back again for the well.
What would a tree be that never stopped its growing,
never left the well?

How do we return to this well-ness, in our businesses and schools, communities and healthcare institutions?

vi. Little Things with Profound Effects

There are hundreds of thousands of books about change—spiritual, operational, and everything in between. While this body of work has yielded some wonderful results, in working with leadership over the past several years I have been concerned with the slow adoption rates of these new practices, and the often disappointingly slow to no apparent change; we seem a bit stuck. In trying to understand why profound change is so hard to achieve, it has often been suggested to me (mostly by friends who work outside of business, in the arts) that we may be thinking too much—over-thinking, over-analyzing, and over-structuring. We might, instead, try to clear out all the noise of complex processes and systems we have artificially manufactured, and instead focus on what comes naturally.

We have all experienced sudden moments of acute clarity or heightened consciousness, often sparked by seemingly trivial or small events—the particular quality of light on a sunny afternoon; a few words uttered by a loved one or close friend; an image on the evening news. That we experience these moments of height-

ened clarity infrequently is a result of the noise in our lives, the constant busy-ness, as well as the years of training to focus on activity rather than essence. Yet, the capacity for such clarity and connection to what is most important—really— is within us, and can easily be tapped by simply re-tuning our selves. While some might suggest years of deep spiritual work or extended sabbaticals might be required, my experience is that some very simple, **little things** can make a huge difference in the quality of our being, as individuals and collectives. These little things take very little time, little to no money or resources (other than our selves showing up, willing participants), yet can have significant results.

This little book captures some of the concepts and methods I have used, primarily with executive leadership, that have opened gateways to new ways of being, and in ways that seem to *stick*. I offer these concepts and methods, along with many concrete examples, for use or adaptation by leaders in public and private sectors who wish to effect systemic and sustainable change.

CHECKLIST

What to Bring Each Day to Summer Music Camp

1. *Your instrument in good working condition*
2. *An open, respectful attitude*
3. *A willingness to learn and try new things*
4. *Smiles and laughter*
5. *A snack*

Interlude

MUSICAL

Penmar Park (excerpt)

(Lights shift; brief ensemble scene down front, facing out: twelve faces of children of all different colors, shapes, and expressions. The poem-song is like chanting to the rhythm of jumping rope.)

"Mama Says"

ENSEMBLE:

Mama says:

Don't dribble the ball
while you're crossing the street
Brush your teeth
Wipe your feet
Don't kiss boys
Don't get laid
You'll get AIDS
Wash your hands
before you eat

Read a book
Do your homework
Watch the news
No rated R TV

Don't get shot
Don't get high

Don't get caught
You'll get beat

The cops are your friends
(Long as you're white)

Don't lie
Don't kill
Don't steal
Don't cheat—

Aw, Mom,
Even the Dali Lama admitted he cheated once or
twice when he was young!

(Blackout.)

The Way In

Putting the People Back in Purpose

Somewhere along the way, we got the idea that work should be somehow socially different than the rest of life—that concern for well-being, relationships, dreams had no place in the workplace or in our schools, medical establishments, and government halls, and instead the human side of our being should be subjugated to task, to the execution of the work itself. Work developed its own rules and sets of relationships, quite outside of familial or community ways of being. Moreover, work came to have its own reason for being, its own purpose, outside of us: in business, typically for the generation of profit; in education, for the achievement of rigidly defined academic standards; in government and civil society, for power. The people, whether customers, employees, patients, students, or citizens, were left out of the purpose equation—so much so that whole bodies of theory and practice have had to be reinvented to remind us of the fact of them! That these so-called "customer-oriented" (or "student-centered" or "patient-centered") movements often fail to change results is an indicator that more than a reminder is needed. We need to reinsert humanity into the purpose of work. The sudden increase in the number of non-governmental organizations (NGOs), now

estimated at over 28,000 worldwide, seems to indicate a growing desire for humanitarian work. Yet, the people-purposes are often obscured in the face of daily challenges—wading through a sea of bureaucratic and economic obstacles causes us to place our attention on the execution of even the most routine tasks, on process, not people. How do we move the real work—that which serves people—back to the center of our attention, and keep it there?

It has been widely held that over-emphasis on external facets of work—the structures, processes, technologies, and tasks we perform—are the result of long-held, deeply ingrained mental models (world views) that were developed in the sciences by Descartes and Newton, and embedded during the Industrial Revolution, the "machine age". Institutions were designed based on machine-like views of how life was thought to function—parts that could be configured to produce certain results; and in the process, humanity was left out. Religious institutions and the dwindling arts were the only surviving mainstream collective domains for humanity to know and grapple with itself. Because neither religion nor the arts have tended to wield global power equal to what has been produced via capitalism and big business, our attention has shifted even more to work and the results it produces, that which produces wealth. As we struggle to deal with the complexity of results-producing work in an evermore complex global economy, amid the often turbulent interrelationships among nation states and their unpredictable societies, the response has often been to step up the pressure by trying to eek out increasing amounts of productivity (more results) with fewer resources. Whether in business or education, government or non-governmental agencies, there are few who are escaping the extreme cost-cutting and resource constraints now widely deployed. The price we are paying in terms of the health and well-being of people has been enormous, and shows no signs of diminishing. Yet it is hard to find a leader in any of these institutions who believes the current practices are sustainable.

New Forms to Follow New Functions

While the mechanistic practices developed during the Industrial Revolution might have served the nature of work during that time well, the world has changed quite a lot since then. Science has long since moved on from Descartes' machine world, yet the majority of us in other fields have not. Why should we expect the practices of the past to work under the very different conditions of the present? Most leaders I talk to today know that our approaches are sorely out of synch with current realities. Yet we persist in emphasizing highly mechanistic structural solutions to solving our problems. While some innovative approaches are being experimented with, these are most often applied on a small scale, and for special projects, not to ongoing work. When trying to improve the performance of large systems, or of the collective who engages regularly in repeating types of work, we tend to rely on the structural solutions. We reengineer processes and policies, restructure organizations and enterprises, outsource and offshore, reconfigure information systems and technologies, and yet with little or no result: over 70% of change initiatives fail. People are picking up the slack, but can hardly be expected to continue doing so at the current rate.

SLIDE

Excerpt from an Executive
Training Seminar

*While top management everywhere is calling for **innovation** and **adaptability**, we tend to rely on hierarchical systems to **try to control behavior**.*

*Hierarchy is rooted in the **mechanistic** view of systems; it is, by design, a **<u>fixed</u> decision-making and control structure**.*

*Hierarchical systems were <u>not</u> intended to enable adaptation and innovation, but **stability***

and **control**.

As we have learned about the principles of living systems in nature, we have begun to see our organizations as **living systems**.

People are not machines that can be controlled.

[**Facilitator Note:** Surprisingly, when this was delivered to executives, they all heartily agreed.]

The old saying goes: "form follows function". Our functions have changed, yet our forms have not. We talk about the age of the knowledge worker, yet organize people as if they were working on a nineteenth century manufacturing assembly line. We advocate innovation and adaptability to enable us to better respond to rapidly changing and often large-scale shifts in the global environment, yet continue to employ hierarchical authority and command-and-control modes of management that are completely antithetical to change and the creative capacity in us required to adapt and innovate. While most leaders acknowledge this contradiction in their approaches versus the outcomes they wish to generate, the question remains: to what extent are they willing to give up control, and what does this letting go imply in terms of the role of leaders in organizations today?

The work being conducted to develop new forms to serve our new functions seems to be yielding some hopeful alternatives to the prevailing hierarchical structures in place in most large institutions today. Building on the concepts of self-organization as explored through contemporary sciences, the phenomena of "social networks" that arise outside of formal structure is being widely explored as a new means of organization that might circumvent the limitations of hierarchical structure. More recently, the concept of **"hastily-formed networks"** seem to be breaking the command-and-control, machine view by advocating minimal

structure that would give the flexibility needed for humans to adapt and innovate.

RESEARCH

Hastily-formed Networks

*Hastily-formed network (HFN) is a term coined by the Naval Postgraduate School to describe the multi-organization groups that come together to create coordinated action in crises, such as hurricane Katrina, the December 2004 tsunami, and the September 11, 2001, attack on the World Trade Center. These multiple groups—the firefighters and police officers, the military and local government, civilians and non-governmental agencies—must somehow quickly mobilize in response to crises. The challenge for HFN is that all of the different groups of responders must be able to take "coordinated action" **collectively**, to adapt and innovate under rapidly changing, uncertain conditions, and to do so **without centralized authority**, and without a common set of information, skills, protocols, and processes. Whereas most responders operate well within their own hierarchical structures, analysis of disaster response efforts reveals that collaboration across groups is often ineffective or absent.*

Disaster response is only one example of a situation in which multiple organizations must respond to a shared challenge; HFN occur in many other contexts as well—whenever cross-functional, cross-company, or cross-sector groups must take "coordinated action" in response to a new, unfamiliar challenge, and somehow generate an innovation that enables them to deal with the challenge. The question being explored is: what can we learn from the alternative structures and types of leadership being developed for HFN so as to enable

adaptive and innovative coordinated action within and across our own institutions? In exploring that question, members of a global learning community, Society for Organizational Learning, in conjunction with researchers from the Naval Post Graduate School, formed two hypotheses:

Minimal structures can better enable both self-organization and coordinated action; generative systems can transcend context.

A system (defined here as the set of language, roles, structures, processes, and practices that organize individual and collective action) can fail when key elements are missing, such as when infrastructure is damaged by a natural disaster, or when several subsystems are combined but operate independently of one another—parts without a whole. One tragic example is recounted in Peter Denning's research about HFN, in which he describes analysis of the disaster response efforts after the attack on the World Trade Center: New York Police Department (NYPD) helicopters that had been monitoring conditions by circling the towers had observed signs of structural collapse in the North Tower and immediately issued an emergency evacuation order to all police; however, they failed to inform the firefighters, who, having had no warning, were not evacuated. There's no doubt that both the NYPD and the firefighters performed heroically, beyond what most of us might imagine possible. And, by most accounts, the command-and-control hierarchies that governed each independently also functioned quite well in guiding independent action. The example raises the question, however, about how to shift independent

action to interdependent collaboration across groups when there is no super-structure to support it. *The same question applies to corporations, governments, schools, and healthcare systems, where complex webs of multi-stakeholder relationships are needed to design, produce, and deliver products or services, in ways that can require a high degree of innovation to deal with often sudden and large-scale changes in policy, technology, funding, consumer preferences, and societal or competitive dynamics, or when persisting challenges require the collaboration of multiple institutions.*

Fixed structures provide clarity and order, but usually only within the finite contexts for which they were designed; they can easily fail us when new conditions arise, catastrophic or otherwise. They are contextually confined. As many of us have experienced in business, contexts like globalization present an ever-evolving and highly complex challenge on a scale that traditionally centralized structures struggle to address. Fixed structures also typically operate via centralized, hierarchical authority; when multiple stakeholder groups are needed, there is no central authority, rendering the whole less effective. Attempts at creating superstructures that can govern multiple stakeholder groups often fail, as we saw with the US Federal Emergency Management Agency (FEMA) in its efforts to coordinate interagency action during the response to hurricane Katrina— an abominable failure that resulted in delayed relief and unnecessary loss of life. Although improvements to superstructures like FEMA can no doubt be made, the feeling is that the inherent

limits of hierarchical structures may continue to impede multi-stakeholder response. Thus, rather than overlaying superstructures to govern multiple stakeholders, the hypothesis is that employing minimal structures such as those used in improvisatory systems in the arts might enable greater degrees of self-organization and adaptability to new contexts.

Enhanced performance of multi-stakeholder systems must occur on both the individual and collective levels.

Implicit in this hypothesis is the assumption that systemic transformation is dependent upon personal transformation. Dispensing with the familiar roles, structures, and rules in order to enable new forms to emerge can require deep personal will and courage, as well as new ways of being as a collective. The challenge here is that our mental models and, consequently, our actions have been shaped by mechanistic systems, often from our early school-age years and continuing through most of our professional lives. Our behaviors become habituated, deeply embedded, making personal change very difficult. We will need to do deep work in "de-mechanizing" our selves in order to participate in a large, dynamic, and generative field of change.

NB: The above is taken from an article I wrote that was originally published by the Society for Organization Learning (SoL) in their May 2006 Reflections journal, based on work I conducted with members of the SoL community and NPS, inspired by the research of Peter Denning at NPS.

Whether crises are defined by temporary catastrophic events like natural disasters, or the often more subtle but persisting crises that plague many of our communities, businesses, schools, and healthcare systems, what is perhaps most interesting about the HFN research is the emphasis on **both** the structural and the personal dimensions of large system change.

While the exploration of minimal structures in HFN may yield some hopeful alternatives to the use of fixed structures and hierarchical controls to govern collective action, the structural starting point in isolation of the personal dimension would be suspect. Structure, no matter how fixed or fluid, echoes the very machine mental models we wish to dispel in that it starts from the external manifestations of relationship (structure), when a more human-centered approach might start from within. Indeed, as the story of student response in the wake of the shooting of Eddie Lopez indicates, profound collective transformation and innovation tend to arise in the **absence** of structure, because it is absent. In some cases, such as the disaster response efforts during the World Trade Center tragedy, it is the structure that was intended to ensure control that caused the breakdown—had the NYPD been trained and accustomed to working not in their functional agency silos but rather as collaborative units with other responders, they might

have thought to warn the firefighters in time. While we tend to see structures as devices to help us work together, they more often than not enforce unintentional **walls that divide us**, physically, mentally, and spiritually.

REPLAY

A Boy Was Shot and Killed Today

Another boy was shot and killed today, this time a seventeen year-old student at Venice High School in Los Angeles, shot dead in the faculty parking lot just after the bell rang, a few miles away from the place where Eddie was shot just a few months ago. The helicopters were circling the neighborhood all afternoon, trying to track down the shooter, the drone of their blades beating the air sounding the all-too-familiar alarm through the neighborhood—choppers circle like that only when hunting down a criminal. People stayed inside; word got out it was a gang shooting, and retaliation was (again) feared. The gangs that were supposedly involved were both mixed-race; so much for assimilation.

*The newspaper reporters captured a picture of the scene at the school: uniformed officers confronting a distraught high school principal, students and parents streaming tears in the background, EMTs carrying the body away, again too late. The whole of the community system was there, frozen in collective time and space for that instant, recorded for the morning paper, a comforting illusion of a reality that does not persist when the crisis is over—the same cast of characters always shows up, but then they all go off back to their respective institutions, as if they didn't inhabit the same **play**, as if all the **scenes** they had each independently enacted didn't somehow all lead to the same*

inevitable climax. And the end of the story never changes. But back they go, to each chip away as best they can at a problem that has been plaguing the city since the 1940s, with no apparent progress. Needless to say, the current methods aren't working. The fact that the problems are extremely complex is a common excuse; tell it to the parents of the dead boy. The territories marked by the police station and school, local government offices and the impenetrable and invisible healthcare, are every bit as guarded as the territories enforced by gangs. Maybe it's time to tear down the walls.

The View from the Middle of the Mess

We are stuck in the structural quagmire of messes of our own making. When you're stuck, the view from the middle of the quagmire doesn't change much. So we keep re-enacting the same rituals, perhaps with some minor adjustments, over and over as if somehow the mere repetition will change the outcome. But, of course, it doesn't. The view from the middle of the mess takes us over, so we see only the challenges at hand, the crises to handle. We end up channeling so much of our attention, time, and resources into dealing with the complex web of obstacles in the existing quagmire that we have little or no space left to try to figure out how to get ourselves out of it, once and for all. We spend our time "putting out fires" and applying band aids that don't solve the problem, but merely (hopefully) keep it from getting worse. When confronted with the same harsh realities day after day, we reinforce the very mental models that keep us stuck—we can't *see* alternatives that might get us out of the mess, and develop literal blind spots. Then we retreat, trying to deal with the pieces of the

whole that seem manageable—a little change here, an improvement there. These improvements, no doubt, can make a difference. But when what we have been doing in bits and pieces to effect change isn't working (i.e., the same messes persist), we're forced again to try to tackle the whole darn thing!

One way to shift the view from the middle of the mess is to look at the many parts of the whole system, and try to understand how each part affects the other, and the health of the whole. This approach, known as systems thinking, has been an evolving practice for some time, with some wonderful results. Leaders in business who practice systems thinking are learning to see the complex interdependencies among different departments, work groups, or processes, and to use that knowledge to approach change, not by trying to fix problems in isolation, but by dealing with the *whole* in ways that can strengthen the parts. Likewise, in large social system change efforts, such as in education system reform, leaders of schools, local governments, law enforcement, and student advocate groups are working together across institutional boundaries to try to address systemic issues, such as low performance of segments of the student population. Yet the cases where these multi-stakeholder initiatives succeed—or, are even attempted—are all too few. Why? Focusing on purely structural solutions from within the current reality can reinforce the same mental models that have been producing limiting results. The second we start to use words that define current structures and systems—"school", or "government", "law enforcement", or "medical center", for example—we often inadvertently put up institutional walls that inhibit whole system change. And, just like the well-intended NYPD in response to the World Trade Center Disaster, the very structure we act within limits our *seeing* of the situation to our own, narrowly defined roles—we respond in terms of function or agency, through practices designed for us alone. While systems thinking helps us to see all the interrelationships among the various parts of a system, seeing these doesn't necessarily help us behave any differently. We simply do not know how to perform as

an ensemble of players, each within his or her own role, to enact a shared *play*. In systems where crises persist for long periods of time, our mental models about "the way things are" take hold, and we inadvertently either reinforce or invent the very obstacles we wish to overcome. In systems where there is conflict among the leaders of different institutions, often the natural impulse is to shore up the walls! Thus, perhaps we need to learn to see the quagmire not only from the point of view of *outside* the system, looking in, but also from *inside* our first-person experience of it, looking out. And, before attempting to fix the structures that guide our interaction, perhaps we need to begin by building the **relationships** needed to carry us across existing boundaries.

ANECDOTES

Playing Nice Versus Taking Your Toys and Going Home

A friend of mine was head of housing for the city of Los Angeles when the devastating Northridge earthquake hit. With over 50,000 housing units damaged or destroyed, their response was deemed a success. He was recently asked by city officials what it was about their response to the disaster that worked so well, and he commented, "The Northridge housing response was effective because it bypassed the rigid bureaucratic structures and operated through a fast-growing organic network based on relationships and individual initiative. Key people, from the lowest echelon, stepped up to respond to myriad issues, and resolved them through creativity and personal connections to other departments (police, fire, building and safety), public sector entities (banks, consultants, associations), and the federal government (HUD and the Clinton Administration). The key organizational structure was a large conference table in the General Manager's

office. Anyone who was active and effective would join in meetings at the table. Technology was primitive. There was no email. Cell phones worked intermittently and were not in general use. Key staff had pagers. The most important communication device was the land line telephone. The most important vehicle for communicating to groups was the squawk box. People that were effective were those that had extensive relationships and good communication skills and who would pick up the phone to reach out to anyone in any agency and be tenacious about it.”

Another friend, an engineer who was involved in a large-scale, multi-sector, multi-country disaster response simulation, described a very different response. Many of the world's leading technology and communications companies had been invited to participate in the simulation, for the purpose of testing and strengthening communications abilities in austere conditions, where power was down and existing systems either non-functioning or severely strained by new demands. He explained that some vendors, whose solutions weren't working, literally "took their toys and went home". (It is interesting to note that the first technology to work was the Hamm radio.) Those who stayed to continue the simulation, rather than collaborate with competitors to come up with a joint solution, literally "stood with their backs to each other".

In reflecting on what he had observed during the simulation, my engineering friend said that one of the most important factors in determining the success or failure of situations where multiple institutions are involved is "leadership". In commenting about the Northridge response, my housing friend later said, "We were practicing HFN management without the computer networks. It still worked—for a while. Then

*order triumphed over organic process and we returned
to 'business as usual'."*

We all know of or have experienced both the successes and
failures of multiple groups coming together to deal with a challenge. Yet, we don't seem to know much about the variables that
affect success—it's safe to say the answer is probably not limited
to technology! How do we create spaces where people deny the
tendency to "take their toys and go home"? How do we get groups
in conflict or even simple avoidance to bring their "toys" to the
table to begin with? And when we do overcome boundaries and
work together to solve a shared problem, what does it take to sustain those relationships and heightened ways of being, to avoid
returning to "business as usual"? For me and many others who
deal in situations of persisting crises, the "leadership" and "relationship" questions are also central. So, many of us have started
asking ourselves:

- What types of leadership are required to forge relationships across institutional or constituent boundaries?

- When effective in working collaboratively for even a
  short while, whether in response to crisis or through
  a special project, what is needed to sustain those
  relationships over time?

- If leaders are defined as anyone who shows up at the
  "conference table", what can we do to prepare them
  and ourselves for the challenge—before, during,
  and after crises?

The Starting Point: Inside-Out

While the exterior structures of our processes, technologies, rules, and roles can't be ignored, when we as leaders approach challenges from in the middle of the structural quagmire it is a heck of a lot harder to get out of it, to get unstuck. And, when we lack the basis for the relationships needed to address whole system challenges, whether because of conflict, competition, or simply lack of habit, many of us often prefer to "take our toys home" rather than try to work out the new structures that are needed. So the question for me is increasingly about what is the right starting point in trying to help ourselves enable whole system change? While our tendency (and, for most of us, our training and management-driven mandate) is to start with the exteriors, the structural solutions, the first step might be to remove ourselves from the noise of external embodiments of the current situation, to open our field of vision and allow new ways of seeing, fresh perspective—not just from the head, but also from the heart. Likewise, making the assumption that the current structures are to blame may be misleading; rather than focusing on changing the structures and systems, maybe it's we who inhabit them that first need to change.

When we focus on the externalized embodiments of reality, we objectify it and, hence, remove it from ourselves—as if what we see has come to be of its own accord! We create the realities. We are not victims of them, nor unwitting observers, but co-conspirators, intentionally or not. So, maybe the work is not about changing The System, but rather about opening our selves to new ways of being, and thus to new ways of being together that might allow us to work as a collective, without artificial control, and in harmony with the real work at hand. To shift the way into the work, maybe we need to stop telling stories about our current realities from a third-person perspective, and instead shift into first-person. Maybe our new stories would not even assume the current structures, roles, and practices we know now—the exteri-

ors we see, the institutions that literally house our practices and embed (institutionalize) our current ways of being. Thus, perhaps our new stories could begin with the interiors—what we need (sustenance), what we want (desires and dreams), and what we will (actions we are determined to take). Starting from the simple source of need, want, and will, we can open our seeing beyond all the noise and frustrations of current reality, and get to the heart of the matter. This simple grounding of reality back in our selves can surface the real work to be done, create true empowerment (where we are actors, not spectators), and move our attention from the often forgotten periphery (oh yeah, that's why we're here), to the center—oh yes, that's why we're here! We can then build from that center, working from the inside-out, to devise the structures, roles, and practices that are needed for real, sustainable change.

QUOTE

William O'Brien

"The success of an intervention depends on the interior condition of the intervener."

While both the structural and the personal aspects of transformation are deemed by thought leaders to be necessary to any sustained change, (as Peter Senge describes, "two sides of the same coin"), it has been suggested that we must start with the self, with the *interior*, as a prerequisite to changing the system, the exterior. Many people I talk to about personal transformation balk at the notion of making the self a priority—sure, leaders can and should always try to develop their leadership capabilities, but command of leadership skill and characteristics is, after all, expected! Others seem to envision forays into squishy self-help or otherwise "self-indulgent" activities, equally unappetizing and invalid, in their views. (I confess that when I first started this work, I shared the

same skepticism!) However, there are a few very practical reasons why focus on our interior conditions makes sense:

1. Our *habits* hardwire us into limited ways of being.

- We all develop deeply ingrained habits that effect what we perceive, and, thus, what we do. Habits are based on past experiences, so when conditions change and our habits have not, we are literally blinded by the limits of our seeing, and cannot act in harmony with new conditions.
- That we develop habits is not due to weakness, but part of our physiological make-up—to perform even the simplest functions, like walking, our brains must weed out a host of sensory inputs and prioritize what is necessary for us to walk. Likewise, our brains construct similar hierarchies of importance based on more complex functions—leading a group of people, for example. Hierarchical constructs are based on what we have learned and repeated over time; it takes a lot of new experiences to break our habits and in a way that can change our ingrained hierarchies! So when external conditions change, even the best of us are often slow to see the new reality, much less respond to it.
- The structures we embed in the institutions we lead are a reflection of our own habits; and, at the same time, the external structures reinforce our habits, even those we wish to break!
- The habits we repeat as leaders set the tone and culture of the organizations we lead; thus, our own personal limits get embedded in the collective. If we can change our habits, it is far likelier that our organizations can change theirs!
- We can intentionally break our habits so as to open ourselves to new ways of seeing and, thus, to new

behaviors and, eventually, new structures. The methods are not hard; but they do require the discipline of practice.

2. We base self-worth on what we know, on the fact of our _knowing_.

- We are conditioned through schooling and cultural norms (in most developed nations, anyway) to expect certainty—that we can use our past experiences and reason to predict likely outcomes. We thus value knowing and those who apparently "know" more than the rest of us.

- In most large institutions, the expectation of everyone from stockholders to employees, or officials to citizens, seems to be that senior leaders have the right "answers"; to admit not knowing what the answers are would be in many cases political suicide!

- When we convince ourselves that we "know", we do not leave ourselves open to learning, to the joy of discovery. Likewise, when we convince ourselves that our knowing is superior to what others claim to know, when different from our perceptions, we are reduced to a battle of who's right and who's wrong, and can hardly expect to collaborate on shared areas of concern.

- Complexity Theory and related modern science, as well as our own empirical experience in the twenty-first century, demonstrate that there is no certainty, that the future cannot be predicted. How, then, can we get comfortable with uncertainty and with differing perceptions of reality, with shifting our sense of self-worth and power from "knowing", to instead being comfortable with not knowing and the joy of discovery?

3. **We are most comfortable working in *silos* — our own, independent function or department, our own industry or agency, our own sector (business, government, civil).**

- While we have generally accepted silos to be a bad thing, for many, experiences in trying to work collaboratively across functions, institutions, or sectors are more often than not frustrating, time-consuming, and ineffectual—while we know in our heads that change across the whole system is needed in order to make change within our own domains, we simply do not know how to work as a true collective, across our silos.

- Our structures hardwire us into silos, reinforcing independent rather than interdependent habits—even matrix organizations are still fixed within topic-specific domains, and the fact that non-governmental or non-profit agencies are segregated by function (education, healthcare, housing, etc.) creates the same silo mindsets.

- While we can change our structures, the hypothesis is that these change efforts typically fail because we have not learned as individuals and groups to operate as whole-system collectives.

4. **We like to hold onto *territory* and *power* over others.**

- As leaders, given current hierarchical and related power structures in place for most institutions today, only we at the top have the access and authority to attempt systemic change, and yet we tend to protect our territories, making systemic collaboration very difficult. The mark of great leadership might be seen as creating a space for change that others are inspired to participate within.

- When I have told the story about the shooting of Eddie Lopez to executives, the thing which seems to most stand out is the fact of Eddie—how is it that a fifteen year-old son of immigrants, with the decks stacked against him, could create such a space around himself that others were inspired to join in it, even after his death? The suggestion is that any one of us, regardless of our circumstances, can shift this sense of space in ways that transform not only our selves, but also invite others to operate from a different space themselves.
- In order to create a space that allows different ways of being, we who own the territories need to give them up and instead become masters at creating "cocoons", safe places where people can take the risk of exploring new ways of being and working, and yet that are permeable, open to others and allowing people to come and go.

QUOTE

Nelson Mandela

"Our deepest fear is not that we are inadequate. Our deepest fear is that we are powerful beyond measure. It is our light, not our darkness that most frightens us. We ask ourselves, who am I to be brilliant, gorgeous, talented, and fabulous? Actually, who are you not to be? ...As we let our own light shine, we consciously give other people permission to do the same. As we are liberated from our own fear, our presence automatically liberates others."

5. We invest in *fortresses*: physical infrastructure, technologies, processes, as if these will make us strong.

- Strength comes not from the fortresses we build, but rather from within.
- The invisible power within us that generates the most profound acts of change, personal and systemic, seems to come from a very strong, crystal clear sense of will—that which propels us into action, as individuals and collectives.

The suggestion here is that we shift our attention to the interior condition that gives rise to action, and let what forms are needed arise from that, rather than trying to manufacture forms in isolation, then trying to make them fit ourselves and our ever-changing conditions. This essential shift in focus means changing our starting point, the way we approach challenges, rather than working from the *outside-in* to instead work from the *inside-out*.

Collective Interiors

It's one thing to deal with the interior of the self in isolation (if such a thing is possible); it's another to surface the collective interior to drive collective action. Processes and structures don't create coordinated action, people do. As the stories about HFN and the kids at my daughter's school illustrate, collective action of a kind that transforms a whole system doesn't tend to happen within fixed structures, and rarely in those governed by centralized authority. What is it about crises that allow large groups of people to self-organize to adapt and innovate, in the absence of authority and pre-defined rules, roles, and processes?

First, there is a very clear and shared sense of a common situation.

When I ask people what they think allows coordinated collective action, most respond by saying they think it is due to a shared sense of purpose. But I think something more basic happens first: the situation itself establishes the context for action, the reason to engage—often even before we translate the act of engagement into explicit ideas about "purpose" or "vision". Situation drives our most basic sense of need. If we are hungry, we do not first step back to define a grand purpose that might cause us to find food; we respond simply with the need to eat. Likewise, if something terrible happens, like the shooting of a friend, we respond first with a basic need to somehow come to terms with the fact, to find or give comfort, or honor our friend. In the workplace, the situation which requires our action often becomes removed from us, an abstraction "out there", or an abstractly defined set of conditions—business targets to hit, academic standards to meet, policies to uphold. This distancing makes it very hard for large numbers of people to rally around shared goals. A shared and immediate, visceral sense of the situation allows us to engage more fully and often more spontaneously as a collective.

Situation includes time, place, events, and people: the current and historical context, the physical conditions and setting, the events and actions, and the people involved including the nature of their relationships to one another. For example, the situation my daughter's classmates encountered was this: in March of 2006, after decades of racial strife and often violent conflict among LA gangs (time and historical context), in a school of 3500 students in the LA area (place), one of the school's beloved students was shot and killed in

a gang drive-by (events), an accidental death that sent a shockwave through the entire community, affecting equally all ethnic groups and local gangs that inhabited the school, many of whom had previously seen only their differences and had avoided one another except in moments when conflict erupted (people). What's important to note is that the situation itself inspired action—not some externally imposed measure of results, process, vision or purpose. If the events or relationships among the people involved had been different, the actions would likely have been different in response. Action is thus directly tied to dealing with the situation, not activities once or twice removed from it. Equally important, everyone who responded to the situation had close physical proximity (they were all students of the same school). Their closeness lent an immediate first-person experience—it affected them on a personal level, even those who didn't know Eddie. Often, in work life, we are physically distanced from the real situation at hand, and thus find it harder to relate to it emotionally, much less respond directly to it. We don't often have emotional clarity in daily life in our institutions. People need meaning, especially shared meaning—we are communal in nature. While developing shared vision can help to link the rational with the emotional reason for action, vision often gets abstracted, especially over time and when people are removed from the tangible "front line" reason that the vision exists. Even if people do connect to vision at first, the connection often weakens over time. People stay engaged through constant interaction with the forces they must contend with to fulfill their purpose, especially when it is based on something larger than themselves. As a situation unfolds, we need to interact within each dynamic moment—this is what makes us

feel alive. Where vision and purpose can become a static picture, situation is an unfolding movie, the outcome of which we cannot know and must continually create. Thus, because a situation is fluid (not fixed, like targets, vision, structure, process, or policy), it causes us to engage all of our selves—head, heart, and hand—to understand what is happening, why, how we feel about it, what we want to do about it, and how to respond. Our perception is heightened because of this demand to continually size up and figure out what to do, as opposed to repeating patterns of prescribed behavior or task—it is inherently more creative.

Most importantly, situation sets the stage for a *shared* context within which we must engage together. It is the shared understanding of a situation that provides a common platform for collective action.

Second, there is deep collective will to engage in the situation—a shared sense of determination that transcends the ordinary, calls us into action.

The nature of crisis causes us to get very quickly to what's most important, and to make choices based on what really matters—the enactment of will. Will is a bit different than intention: intention is what one wants; will is what one is determined to do. Intention is meaningless without the determination of the will to cause us to take action. In the situation at my daughter's school, it can easily be argued that each day the majority of students show up on campus with a clear intention to make it through the day without trouble; yet the intention is not always held, lacking a deeper source of will that would drive them to make the right choices, even when extremely difficult to do so. The peaceful and loving response to the death of Eddie Lopez, within the volatile interracial and gang-related situation,

was clearly an act of will, one that allowed them to transcend old ways of being. What is most compelling is that it was an act of *collective will* that encompassed the entire student body.

Will is based on deep desire, belief, and need, on both the practical and spiritual levels. We all have these things that generate will within us. Yet, it is hard for individuals and groups to hold will because our desires and aspirations often take second priority to basic needs. Whether the need for sustenance, or merely getting through the day, the extent of survival challenges often erode what space we have left for dreams. For those who are engaged in trying to effect complex, large system change—cleaning up the messes—the very will that led them into taking on big challenges sometimes ends up driving them into despair or cynicism. My friend, the former head of housing for Los Angeles, who now builds affordable housing for low income people in the area, reminded me that the best intentions often get a little muddied when you're floating down the sewer with the rest of the sludge in the system! In corporations, we lose our sense of will either because personal vision cannot be reconciled with organizational vision, ("personal" being defined generally, often outside of work, encompassing all of life in ways traditional organizational vision does not—in which case the only alternative is to quit), or because the voice of our will becomes obscured by all the noise of objectives, processes, and systems. No matter how well-aligned, once personal and organizational vision lose their original intent, we start focusing on them as subjects of our work, rather than the purpose for which they were originally designed. We may try to force ourselves into compliance, but forced-will is hard to sustain, especially under extreme pressure and for long

periods of time. So we withdraw, go through the motions, only giving a small part of ourselves to get by.

I believe that much of the difficulty in holding one's own will is due to the tendency to isolate ourselves from the collective. Leaders think in terms of their own intentions, their own vision, and those few who manage to live by their will are usually deemed to be heroes. Most of us, however, are not heroic, at least not for sustained periods of time! But maybe we don't have to be. It is said that to attempt large-scale change alone is folly, but that a few determined people can change the world. I don't know how many people it takes; but I do believe it is through connection to collective will, based on the shared context of a common situation that we all care about, that causes profound transformation.

Collective will is the ***"attractor"*** that allows form to emerge from ***chaos***. It is an organizing principle that allows us to take collective action in harmony with an unpredictable, ever-changing situation, in the absence of centralized authority or fixed structure and process. Many of the methods described later in this book are based on this hypothesis.

SCIENCE

Attractor

In dynamical systems, an attractor is a set to which the system evolves after a long enough time.

Chaos

Chaos derives from the Greek and typically refers to unpredictability. In the metaphysical sense, it is the opposite of law and order: unrestrictive, both creative

and destructive. The word did not mean "disorder" in classical-period ancient Greece. It meant "the primal emptiness, space".
Source: Wikipedia

Third, there are no structural obstacles—people are free to do what is needed, unencumbered by formal rules and protocols.

Disaster or crisis is often characterized by sudden loss of the familiar—physical infrastructure, like roads and communication systems, and relational structures and roles, even people we love or have come to rely upon. Organizations are intentionally designed to avoid such crises, to control. But the structures and processes and policies we make create only the illusion of control—living systems of people cannot be controlled. When structures are fixed, we are inhibited from adapting to evolving needs in a situation. Furthermore, structures create walls that divide us— and then necessitate the use of other artificial means like vision or purpose to try to patch us back together again! As pointed out previously, the time and energy it takes to manage structures and processes diverts us from the real work at hand, the enactment of will. The absence of external structures ("chaos" in the Greek sense), allows us to move the real work to the *center*, and then to self-organize whatever forms are needed based on what matters most.

Fourth, we remember we need each other—not soloists but ensemble performers.

There's nothing like a crisis to remind us we are not enough alone. My friend who was the head of housing for LA when the Northridge earthquake hit,

said the first thing you think of in a situation like that is: "Okay, who do we need to reach out to." Likewise, as soon as word got out about the shooting of Eddie Lopez, the first thing the kids did was reach out to each other, organizing a host of activities across the spectrum of the formal school groups (that typically did not collaborate with one another). Yet under what circumstances is one person or specialized group enough to deal with the situation alone? The collective is almost always required, whether we acknowledge that fact or not. The only difference between a state of crisis and "normal" conditions may be that the rate at which our familiar routines and ways of being are disrupted is greater during crisis than the rate at which we ordinarily decay! Crisis merely makes our limitations evident and undeniable. We are never enough alone.

Remembering that we are not enough alone causes a profound shift in the way we view ourselves—we are suddenly not solo performers, the masters of our independent domains, but rather members of an ensemble, a group of people who must collaborate in order to make a "shared song". In the daily life of institutions, pre-defined roles and structures govern how we interact, often isolating us—and we lose each other. In crisis, we are forced to step outside of formal structures and to take on new or different roles that allow us to work as a true collective, and usually find we can. Our difficulty in doing this under ordinary circumstances may have something to do with how we typically define our roles. In order for collectives to function, we usually need a very clear definition and shared understanding of individual roles. However, in crisis, role definitions are based on the needs of the situation, not protocols and traditions, and not organization

charts! Every institution has its role definitions, usually a mix of hierarchical roles governing decision making and functional roles covering needed areas of expertise. Yet, when these roles are fixed, they can limit interaction. In high-performing self-organizing groups, people take on different roles naturally, to make the group function. Some of these roles are based on subject matter expertise or technical skill, and others on relational skills. In most organizations, however, roles are often limited to areas of functional or topical expertise—even so-called "generalists" are those who are supposed experts in management (meaning others aren't supposed to take that role). In crisis, we certainly need experts—someone who knows how to put out fires, manage emergency communications, provide medical assistance, and so on. However, as the case of the NYPD and firefighters demonstrates, we need to shift from defining roles narrowly in terms of function, task, or chain of command, and to instead see our roles within the context of the whole situation, and as performers in an ensemble, not a solo agency or organization. This requires us to take on new or additional roles, and of a relational nature. And, it requires us to adapt our roles as the situation dictates—from being an expert in setting up communications equipment one minute, to being a communicator or networker who can link people together the next. Note that leadership can and should occur through any role, and all roles. One person can play more than one role, and many people might share the same role, as needed. The challenge is in imagining the types of roles needed, and allowing them to evolve, and, when necessary, to develop the additional capacities or areas of expertise needed, as situations change.

Now, the control-freak in us may say, "We must plan, we must regulate, we must (at least) orchestrate!" Yet, there is no evidence to suggest that hierarchical controls and fixed structures improve outcomes. The capacity to self-organize comes naturally to us; it is merely our ingrained habits that have come of living within rigid structures that create discomfort. Likewise, where we often limit our roles to narrowly defined fields of expertise or certain types of management oversight activities, we all have the capacity to play the relational roles necessary to support collective action. Seeing the roles we play as part of the larger collective, sharing a common will to engage in a common situation, frees us to go back to our natural ways of being. We can easily create new habits that allow us to participate regularly as a true collective—if we want to.

The No-Excuse Clause

Despite attempts throughout history at paying more attention to people (whether well-intended or manipulative in nature—like to get them to be more productive), somewhere along the way priority shifted from sustenance of the community to sustainability of The Institution itself. Now, it can certainly be argued that the majority of our institutions—businesses, governments, and non-governmental organizations—were intended to serve the needs and interests of people, to ensure the well-being of society over-all. And, it can be argued that when our institutions fail to serve people as well as they might, or to serve all people equally well, that the limits are due to the harsh realities and complexities of life, and that we are doing the best that we can at the moment. Maybe that's true. However, that our institutions have evolved toward more **democratic**, humane principles, yet at the same time tend to base decisions on that which generates wealth, often to the detriment of large segments of society and to the environ-

ment, certainly presents a contradiction between our ideals and our actions.

THESAURUS

democratic

free
classless
equal
open
unrestrictive
(antonym) *repressive*

This apparent contradiction between the ideals of democracy and the actuality of self-proclaimed democracies, some say, is the result of human nature. While it may be hard to find people who would say they don't wish for the betterment of humanity overall, many maintain that "life simply isn't fair", and that it is human nature to protect what we have, to get what we can get, even when it means taking it from others or fighting others who we believe are trying to take from us. This mental model about the cut-throat aspects of human nature seems to shape our actions—even when our words try to paint a nicer picture! We accept the failure of our institutions to take care of people, all people, because we perceive that *inequity is to be expected.* And we use it as an excuse for sometimes bad and, in the end, impractical behavior—the cost of inequities such as lack of access to good education and healthcare is economically unsustainable. To accept the get-what-you-can, "dog-eat-dog" view of humanity is simply self-defeating. If we insist that our nature will always cause us to behave as we have, how is real change ever possible?

We have been stuck in a very negative view of humanity in part because of the assumptions made by certain scientists, primatologists whose studies of chimpanzees (our closest relatives) sug-

gested that violence in primates (that's us) is innate, mixed with Darwin's notion of "survival of the fittest", whose scientific findings insisted—and caused us to insist—that our base animal nature hardwires us to perform often vile acts to ensure our self-survival. Thankfully, new studies of non-human primates suggest that our nature is actually not all that bad, and that given the right environment, we are prone to behave in generous, humane, and peaceful ways.

And so now we have **no excuse:**

SCIENCE

The Good Monkey Theory

In a study of savanna baboons in Kenya, researchers Dr. Robert Sapolsky of Standford and his colleague, Dr. Lisa Share, discovered that pacifism can be learned, that cultures can change, and that nurturing behaviors can sustain the long-term health of a community—despite the fact of aggression and violence in others—at least in non-human primates. Here's what they observed:

A community of some 62 baboons known as Forest Troop lived in the trees near a tourist lodge in Kenya. The lodge had recently expanded its garbage pit, attracting another group of baboons, Garbage Dump Troop, who took up residence near the pit. The dominant males from Forest Troop decided they wanted to partake of the refuse, so those who were strong and aggressive enough went to fight over the spoils with the members of Garbage Dump Troop, raiding the pit each dawn. The raids and fighting over the garbage went on for some time; baboons are known to fight over food, even in natural settings.

But then, some of the meat in the dump was contaminated with bovine tuberculosis, infecting all who

had eaten it. Most of Garbage Dump Troop died, along with all of the Alpha males from Forest Troop.

However, the females, their young, and about 50% of Forest Troop males who had stayed at home, being too subordinate to attempt fighting at the dump, all survived. With the Alpha males gone, the Forest Troop culture changed, almost overnight: the surviving baboons relaxed their hierarchy, allowing the subordinate males and females alike to thrive, and replaced their customary biting and fighting with the use of affection and mutual grooming. The males, rather than keeping their distance as they often do in baboon troupes, began to hang out with the nurturing females. Instances of aggression, commonly observed between dominant males and their subordinates, all but disappeared. They lived in peace.

Amazingly, Forest Troop has maintained their peaceful, nurturing culture for over two decades now, even though the male survivors of the epidemic have since died and been replaced with other males from the outside, many of them dominant males who were accustomed to getting what they wanted through aggression. It remains uncertain how the transmission of Forest Troop culture to newcomers occurs; but it has been observed that within hours the newly arrived Alpha males settle down and give up their fighting instinct so as to enjoy the low-stress life and the pleasure of affection.

In an interview in the Los Angeles Times, Dr. Frans B.M. de Waal, the director of the Living Links Center at Emory University commented, "The good news for humans is that it looks like peaceful conditions, once established, can be maintained. And, if the baboons can do it, why not us? The bad news is that you might first have to knock out all of the most

aggressive males to get there."

Source: "A Pacific Culture Among Wild Baboons" by Saplosky and Share, published on www.plosbiology.org

I personally have no trouble with the idea of weeding out the Alpha males; the question is how to peaceably do it.

Staying True

I love science; my first heroes as a child were Jane Goodall and Jacques Cousteau. I still love science. But I never take it as objective fact. It's easy enough to see by tracing changes in scientific theory over the centuries how any one scientific advancement is merely a snapshot in time of our evolving perception of what we think we know, a transitory thought in an infinite evolution of ideas that are no more or less "true" than the art of the day—a poet's or painter's interpretation of life at the moment is just as "true" as a theorem or research study. And, I believe, it's only because science makes a lot of money that we continue to hold it up as somehow more "true", more valid than what our artists tell us about life. The arts keep us honest—they do not pretend to be objective, and they come not just from the head (which always fools us into a false sense of certainty and the illusion of control), but also from the heart. The heart allows us to contend with the messiness of life, to fully embrace the complexity of human systems on their own terms, and to thus more effectively engage with each other. Indeed, as we have seen in looking at the wondrous human capacities that surface in crises, we draw from a deeper place in our selves in order to deal with complex challenges—it is the "primal emptiness" of "chaos" that allows both our destructive and creative potentials to emerge. The arts enable us to embrace

the creative impulse that is inherent in chaos, so we can adapt and innovate as a way of being, not as victims of circumstance or crisis.

The arts also provide a "holding space" for collective consciousness, playing back the evolving story of our humanity. While we each experience heightened moments of consciousness, or instances where we find we are able to perform in amazing ways with one another, the difficulty is how to *hold* that state of being when we are still self-defined by an old story of our selves, based on self-limiting images of who we are and what we can be. The arts help us to create new stories about ourselves, an emerging self that can at any moment come into being—arising from whatever messiness exists in current reality—so as to transform both the individual's and collective's identity. Where most other disciplines deal with discreet aspects of our being, the arts are able to hold all of the messy dimensions of self and collective. More than any other discipline, the arts can help us to hold both the current messes and the future we seek to create.

Thus, the remainder of this little book draws not from the sciences (not even management science), but from the arts as a way to tap into our essential nature that is every bit as possible, every bit as "true", as that displayed in our cousins, the baboons of Forest Troop.

Interlude

MUSICAL

Penmar Park (excerpt)

(Homer walks down front center, into a spot.
Music fades in, a Calypso theme…)

"Monkey Theory"

HOMER *(singing):*

Now I have a sad story to tell
About the Monkey Theory
Of the Alpha male
Doctor say
The trouble began
With the Alpha male
Way before man

Monkey male is big as he is mean
Run the jungle like hurricane
Might is right, force is the way
Better fight, or get outta his way
Little monkeys see that to survive
Takes matter over mind
To stay alive

Doctor say
Man don't evolve
Much farther than the monkey
In banana tree
So when war comes

No one sees the possibility
Figure war is just
Inevitability

But doctor say
There's a good disease
Wiped out all the Alpha monkeys
From the banana trees
And the mamas left
Tending their babies
Soon forget
Inevitability
When babies grow up
They don't see
The Alpha males
Always fighting
So when they get big
Instead they play
Monkey fun
Every day

Now Doctor say
Man don't evolve
Much farther than the monkey
In the banana tree
But to this day
They live in peace—
Monkey hope
For the human race

(Blackout.)

Act One:
Ensemble Approaches to Working
from the Inside-Out

Overture:
Many Instruments, Playing a Shared Song

So, it seems that things keep getting worse, and more complex; when our best efforts fail to meet the challenges at hand, people and the planet are increasingly expected to pay the price. And this is not sustainable.

We tend to try to fix the situations by focusing on exteriors—the systems, structures, processes, technologies, and policies that we hope will shape and enable our actions. Yet, profound change seems to occur in the *absence* of these exterior forms.

We think very, very hard, using our heads as best we can. Yet, sustainable change seems to come from a different place, an invisible source within us that is larger than any one of us, and emerges through each of us.

It's hard to hold this space, hard to work together, across all of the physical and relational boundaries that divide us. And while we know in our heads we must act in concert, to change the system as a whole system, to do such a thing is very, very hard—time gets in the way, and distance, and sometimes conflict.

And yet, even when we retreat, we do so knowing we are not enough alone.

And so, it seems we need to learn to act from this source, from the *interior*, on both the individual and collective levels, and then to let what new exterior forms emerge from there: inside-out.

The challenge is to make space for accessing this source, alone and together, and to learn what it is to work together, as an ensemble, where the many instruments can play a shared song.

Ensemble Work

Why is it so hard for us to work together as an ensemble, in other words, all together, as one? As my daughter now approaches the end of her high school years, and has started looking at colleges, I keep an eye out for courses of study that might help prepare her and her generation for working together, in any context—with colleagues at work, with other stakeholders across the systems in which they might work, in daily routines or in crisis. Where are these courses? Outside of performing arts programs, I cannot find them—at least not the ones that help us act from our hearts, not our heads, or from the source of collective aspiration and will, courses that not only offer ideas but allow us to practice this way of being (for ensemble work does take a lot of practice). When I think back to my own schooling, I cannot recall classes that taught us how to work together, much less forums that allowed us to practice learning together. I moved all over the country when I was growing up, yet not one of the primary or secondary schools I attended offered such things, the few music classes and extracurricular sports being the closest thing to it, yet always framed within competitive constructs or rigidly defined roles and rules, and, thus, not really about ensemble at all. And so, I think we so often fail to work well together, across boundaries or despite our differences, in large part because most of us have never learned how to do it. For me, it wasn't until I went to col-

lege and studied theatre and dance that I learned anything at all about what ensemble performance means. Having studied theatre for many years, and having worked professionally within it, I must say I am still learning what it means! But now, I go back to those roots, to see what might be useful to the systems in which I now work, to adapt as a source of learning for corporations and other multi-stakeholder systems and, potentially, to evolve new models that might inform the ways in which large, diverse groups can work together more effectively to create the futures they want. For whether we are dealing with temporary crises or persisting crises, systemic change seems to require a type of leadership and relationship among leaders that is contrary to many of our habits—we are, most of us, either devout or unwitting soloists! For those of us who simply weren't trained to collaborate, whether across functions within a single organization or across institutions within a large system, we may need to re-learn how to work together before we can fully accomplish our goals. In systems where conflict keeps us apart, we first need to find ways to heal the relational wounds before we can attempt change. These relational dimensions of work are, for me, all about performing as an ensemble. The ideas and methods described later in this section of the book are, thus, drawn from practices used in the arts to perform as an ensemble, in ways that draw from the invisible but powerful strength of the collective interior.

From Crisis to Chaos

Ensemble performance is an inherently creative process, one that requires us to draw from a different place in ourselves and to connect to each other in ways that many of us are not accustomed to doing, at least not at work. Creative processes tend to arise in crisis situations because the void a crisis produces requires us to

create something new in the absence of the old. When natural disaster destroys infrastructure, we create new ways of communicating and new relationships; when the death of a beloved schoolmate causes a group of kids in conflict to somehow together honor their lost friend, they create peace; when the violent Alpha males of a monkey tribe are wiped out, the survivors create a more nurturing culture. When groups fail to respond well to crisis—or to any new situation that presents new conditions—it is often because they do not allow themselves to create something new, but rather try to force-fit old protocols and practices into a radically different situation than that for which they were intended. In everyday work life, we put on our blinders so we don't have to deal with change, and, thus, avoid creation in favor of stability and control. Yet, things change, and stasis is death for any system. It is thus very useful to embrace "chaos" and the "destruction" (loss of the familiar) that allows "creation" (the emergence of something new), rather than try to eliminate it. Now, daughter-of-a-civil-engineer that I am, I'm hardly advocating that we create chaos and use destruction to allow creation! However, there are gentle but powerful ways to achieve the same types of transformation by drawing from the age-old ensemble methods employed in the arts. The arts evolved outside of mechanistic control models and their inflexible structures—often in opposition to them. Group art forms such as the performing arts offer a *collective* vehicle for profound transformation by removing us from the familiar, placing us in a shared space of "primal emptiness", contexts where our learned habits and old selves and systems no longer apply, causing us to draw from this source as an ensemble. Ensemble performance in the arts is about people working together to create something out of nothing, to lend meaning where there was none, and to create a shared story that not only captures the essence of current experience, but also advances our dreams and generates the collective will to create what might be. As a group process, ensemble work is designed to help us discover something new, to embrace the unknown and tangle with the unexpected, so as to

continually adapt and innovate.

The creative potential in the "primal emptiness" of chaos is always present, our "well" and also our "blank canvas" to fill with whatever we desire to create. So why not draw from it in more proactive ways, to evolve and grow as we wish?

Now, most of us weren't trained as artists—an MBA or a degree in education or public policy likely didn't provide the kind of training needed to prepare one for this type of work. But, ensemble methods used in the arts are based on a set of competencies that anyone can develop. In life as in art, we are all painters starting from a blank canvas, storytellers confronted with a blank page, performers on an empty stage, drawing from a place in ourselves, with each other, that allows us to create new realities, the future we seek to make.

Ensemble Improvisation as a Means to Innovation and Adaptability

Leaders of all types of institutions, public and private, big and small, have accepted—at least in their heads—that systemic change, especially within complex or dynamic, rapidly changing or unfamiliar contexts, requires us to adapt and innovate in much more nimble and far more transformational ways than ever before. Adaptation and innovation are creative processes. The creative processes used to innovate and adapt under highly complex or rapidly changing, uncertain conditions require us to be able to improvise—to make something up out of nothing, or to deal with new and unfamiliar conditions in new ways.

DEFINITIONS

Innovation, Adaptability, Improvisation

Innovation (*i.e., new ways of adding value [P. Senge]*) and **adaptability** (*i.e., personal and systemic transformation in harmony with changing conditions*) *are the result of group improvisation.*

Improvisation: *a group learning, discovery, and prototyping process, one that is not confined by structure and is not dependent upon hierarchy or centralized control.*

While we know we need to be able to adapt and innovate, most large, complex systems in use today rely on:

- Fixed structures to govern process and relationships
- Hierarchical command-and-control authority to govern decision-making
- Roles defined by preconceived job descriptions and often narrowly defined tasks
- Linear and often slow processes of first planning, then executing fixed plans (or, in more sophisticated systems, adding reflection and learning at points in the process)

Many of these features of large systems today are, obviously, antithetical to innovation and adaptability, as well as to the large-scale, multi-stakeholder response required to transform not just independent parts, but the whole system.

The improvisational systems derived in the arts were developed outside (and even in opposition to) the mechanistic systems of large institutions and large systems. Improvisational art forms, such as jazz and theatre improv, are not based on a fixed piece of

music or a scripted play, but rather an evolving experience that depends on us to create it. These more generative systems were designed to nurture both the self and the collective, to facilitate self-organization and continuous innovation, and to enable deep collaboration in service of collective will. Improvisation in the arts is, by design, a group learning and discovery process, one that is not confined by fixed structure and is not dependent upon hierarchy, and that allows us to draw from the interior, rather than futzing with the exteriors that may or may not serve our will.

Improvisation is based upon a set of interdependent principles that govern individual and collective work.

> **Situation:** *A series of conditions and actions that define the whole, including context (time, place,history, physical and relational conditions), events or conflicts, the key players involved, and the nature of their relationships to one another.*

> **Role:** *The part one plays in effecting the situation.*

> **Ensemble:** *The group of people who together effect the situation, through their interdependent roles,*

> **Intention:** *What one wants and why.*

> **Will:** *What one is determined to do, as expressed through action.*

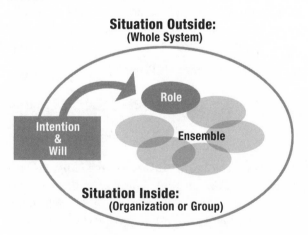

Situation Outside:
(Whole System)

Role

Intention & Will

Ensemble

Situation Inside:
(Organization or Group)

While there are many principles used in different forms of improvisation, those most relevant to the challenge of working from the collective interior include principles based on theatre improvisation. In theatre improvisation, rather than action being guided by a fixed script (i.e., a plan or structure), the actors must together respond to a common but dynamically changing situation, each playing his or her own role within an ensemble, and in ways that enact intention through will (as described above).

Theatre improvisation can thus be used as a group innovation process wherein many different actors, often with diverse or conflicting intentions, act upon the common situation to create new outcomes or to cause new situations to emerge. In institutional settings, the "actors" must also begin with a shared understanding of the situation, both on the outside of the organization or group (the sum of the political, economic, social, technological, or ecological conditions that establish context), and on the inside (the context within the organization or group). The ability to respond to both the larger systemic context and the more immediate internal context is what allows groups to adapt in harmony with changing or highly complex conditions. Improvisation methods used by actors can help develop the capacities needed to "sense" the complex and interdependent conditions in an evolving situation, and to learn how to see role, intention, and will within that dynamic context. It is important to note that, like crisis situations, the shared context of the common situation inspires collective, "coordinated action", and that action derives from deep will, not externally imposed rules, processes, or protocols.

EXAMPLE

Improv Situation

Two brothers are going into a small-town bank, intending to rob it. Both have guns. There is an armed security guard inside, many customers, and a few bank employees. Robber A's intention is to get the money and

escape without getting caught. Robber B was coerced by his older brother, Robber A, to participate in the robbery. Robber B's intention is to make sure no one gets hurt.

Throughout the improv, each actor needs to make choices based on "will", within their respective roles, and the common situation.

Equally important is the reliance on ensemble. As we have seen, fixed structures and processes tend to promote independent action—the structures and processes are designed to connect the actions of different people in a controlled environment, yet through a series of discreet events, like cogs in a machine. Because most structures and processes are intended to limit behavior to predictable and repetitive action within in a controlled environment, these fixed mechanisms inhibit adaptability—it can take a long time to change an organization's structure or to re-engineer processes. In large, multi-stakeholder systems where there are no connections among the structures and processes across institutions, there is no formal means of connecting people around shared challenges. Rather than relying on fixed structures and processes, actors in an ensemble must rely upon each other to co-create action, to self-organize based on relational, not structural, forms

The "attractor" that allows form to emerge from chaos is the common situation, and the individuals' ability to co-create as an ensemble. For many of us trained to perform in institutional settings, it is a big shift to see our respective roles as an interdependent cast of characters needed to perform a common play. We must learn how to allow roles to be guided not by fixed tasks or power structures, but by intention and will. This holistic approach enables large groups of people to enact collective will, to keep the real work front and center, and to innovate so as to adapt to a continually evolving situation. The following competencies and meth-

ods for enacting them are intended to help with these challenges, and to shift individual and collective ways of being.

Requisite Competencies for Ensemble Improvisation

In reflecting on what I have been learning from ongoing HFN research, and my own experimentation using improvisation principles to help leaders perform as ensembles, I keep going back to the same questions:

> What types of leadership are required to forge relationships across institutional and stakeholder boundaries?

> When working collaboratively for even a short while, whether in response to crisis or through a special project, what is needed to sustain those relationships over time?

> If leaders are defined as anyone who shows up at the "conference table", what can we do to prepare them and ourselves for the challenge—before, during, and after crises?

And so, I started to wonder: what type of competencies (i.e., knowledge and skills), are needed for leaders of these complex, multi-stakeholder systems? Having been trained in ensemble performance and improvisation myself, I went back to what my theatre teachers and mentors taught me, and began to distill what competencies seemed most critical, in addition to the usual leadership competency fare, focusing on those required for both individual leaders and groups of leaders to enact the principles of improvisation in ways that effect whole system change. Because I

think people tend to understand the intention of competencies best when they are defined through very specific, tangible, and observable behaviors (i.e., actions), I have tried to crystallize myriad improvisation practices into a few, clear behavioral definitions. As a starting point, this set of competencies and associated behaviors might be defined as follows:

PRINCIPLES	COMPETENCIES & BEHAVIORS

Situation

Pure Observation
- Observes fully using all senses, without characterizing
- Places full attention on the subject of observation or interaction

Shared Perception
- Sees the situation inside of the organization or group in context of all stakeholders and conditions in the whole system
- Describes own perceptions of context, events, and relationships from first-person perspective (emotional, relational, spiritual, physical manifestations)
- Solicits perceptions from all key stakeholders in the system
- Engages stakeholders in dialog to surface shared and differing perceptions
- Crystallizes collective perceptions to move the "real work" to the center of attention
- Holds both shared perceptions and persisting conflicts
- Actively helps to maintain a holding space for the "real work" to be done

Will

Shared Will
- Surfaces individual will based on the common situation and the "real work"
- Surfaces and holds counter-will
- Engages others in synthesizing individual wills to crystallize shared will
- Holds conflicting wills of others with shared will for change

PRINCIPLES	COMPETENCIES & BEHAVIORS

Role

Role Creation and Evolution
- Defines own role in context of the situation, the other roles involved, and the shared will to do the "real work" at hand
- Explores own role through interaction with others
- Evolves own role in ways that consistently demonstrate individual and shared will
- Refines own role to support other roles in effecting the common situation
- Adjusts role as needed based on changes in the situation or other roles

Ensemble

Action Observation and Adjustment
- Continually observes what is happening in the situation, across the whole system, at present (emotional, relational, spiritual, physical manifestations)
- Holds attention on the others in the situation, in each moment of interaction
- Adjusts own actions as needed to affect the present situation and/or to support others in affecting the situation, so as to enact shared will

Imagination
- Imagines what might happen next or in the distant future, based on past events, present events and interactions, and multiple possible outcomes
- Experiments with different choices and actions to continuously explore the present moment and alternatives for effecting change, individually and collectively
- Holds sources of pain and fear, with sources of joy and hope, in embrace of deep discovery
- Instills wonder

Assuming that at least some of these competencies and behaviors are useful in addressing the challenge of systemic change from the collective interior (inside-out), I then asked myself: how do we develop these competencies, and what sorts of methods might help individuals and groups perform the behaviors over time? The remainder of this book attempts to address those questions—at least as a start!

Ensemble Improvisation Methods

Because this book is about about shifting collective interiors to allow for systemic change, the arts-based approaches included are those used to explore collective experience. Included are approaches that I have adapted from two art forms, story and theatre improvisation. Both art forms have been used widely in corporate contexts, but, as I understand it, typically as yet another way of getting groups of people focused on exteriors, like brand, vision, and strategy. The uses of story and theatre improv-based approaches here is a bit different, in that the purpose is to surface and transform collective interiors by first intentionally creating the "void" (the blank sheet or empty stage to fill), and then "presencing" the new story or play that seeks to emerge, unconstrained by old habits and the structural quagmires we've created. In my experience, the results that arise from using these arts-based approaches are truly transformational; but these results come not by focusing on them, but rather by putting attention on the interior, the void that allows the full potential of any one of us or of any group to emerge.

Both story and theatre improv-based approaches are intuitive, part of our collective history and way of being for thousands of years, and, thus, easily accessible to most people. Since the beginning of humans' ability to communicate through speech, story has

been a natural and transforming way of creating collective meaning. Where story in modern times is most often used as a solitary vehicle for reflection, one writer to one reader, it was initially a group experience, and dynamic in nature—both storytellers and audience co-created stories, and they evolved their stories over time according to the evolving experiences of the community. The second art form, theatre improvisation, was an offshoot of early storytelling, where stories were enacted by players—stories on their feet. As with stories, theatre improvisation often unfolds according to the dynamic among the players, as well as between players and audience. The physicalization of experience through theatre allows us to move from the head to the truth that is in the body, our "holding space" for the sum of all our senses and being. The group experience of communal storytelling and theatre improv allows the members of a community to explore their own roles in context of a shared and dynamic situation, as individuals and as an ensemble. Because both story and theatre are creative processes, they can also develop the individual and ensemble skills necessary for adaptive, innovative systems. At their core, they cultivate the prerequisite competencies needed to enact innovation practices, particularly in contexts where rapid change and uncertain futures require groups to adapt on the fly, or where groups are stuck in persisting crises that they cannot seem to overcome.

QUOTE

Augusto Boal

"Theater is the capacity possessed by human beings to observe themselves in action. Humans are capable of seeing themselves in the act of seeing, of thinking their emotions, of being moved by their thoughts. They can see themselves here and imagine themselves there. They can see themselves today and imagine themselves tomorrow. This is why humans are able to identify, rather than merely recognize, themselves and others....

To identify is to be able not only to recognize within the same repetitive context but also to extrapolate to other contexts; to see beyond what the eye sees, to hear beyond what the ear hears, to feel beyond what touches the skin, to think beyond what words mean."

Because one's own instrument must be well-tuned in order to play well within an ensemble, I begin with some methods that help to open the self to new ways of being, and new possibilities. Next, because it is easier for most people to begin by exploring the story of our interior existence in a stationary, reflective mode, these methods begin with using story to surface and integrate diverse perceptions, then move into the more sophisticated and challenging uses of theatre improvisation to both develop and demonstrate ensemble ways of being.

WARNING

Little Movements, Big Shift

I began by suggesting that "little things" can make a huge difference in the quality of our being and, thus, of our doing. The arts-based methods create this "little movement" from the old self to the new, in what is a very subtle but profound shift in both our individual and collective interiors. However, in order for such a shift to occur, we need to be willing to take personal risks, to try out things that may make us feel uncomfortable—indeed, discomfort is a good sign that something is happening in us because it is an indicator that we are actually breaking our old, familiar habits! As leaders, we need to also be willing to try out these new ways of being and engaging with the people we lead, so we can shift the tone and make a "space" that others can feel safe to enter into.

The "little things" are easy enough to make time-space for in the busy-ness of daily life—you can take 15 minutes in a staff meeting, a couple of hours with stakeholders, a day or two with a work group, to try out some of these methods. See what works for you, and then embed those practices into regular, ongoing activities. However, you have to first be willing to make the leap yourself!

De-mechanization Methods: Freeing the Body to Perceive

PRINCIPLE	COMPETENCIES & BEHAVIORS
Situation	**Pure Observation** • Observes fully using all senses, without characterizing

Acting in harmony with changing or highly complex conditions requires us to be able to perceive the whole of the "situation", both outside (in the larger environment in which we operate), and inside the institutions in which we work. Otto Scharmer suggests that the central crisis we face is one of perception—when we cannot perceive all the complex, diverse forces at play, we fail to act in harmony with changing conditions or with the needs of those we intend to serve.

DEFINITION

Perception (noun)

1) information, attitudes, or awareness such as acquired by using the senses to understand the surrounding environment or situation;

2) *the ability to notice or discern things that escape*
the notice of most people

Failure to perceive creates risk; the ability to perceive can often
present significant opportunities. For example, for an automobile
manufacturer operating in the mid to late nineties, the ability to
perceive potential changes in fuel efficiency and emissions regu-
lations might drive a change in engine technology, so as to create
more fuel-efficient and clean vehicles. The ability to perceive
these changes early on could (and did, for some) create a significant competitive advantage. But perception is tricky; we don't
always want to take in information that contradicts our current
ways of thinking or causes us to make big changes in what we're
currently doing. In the case of the automotive industry, one group
of executives I worked with, armed with mountains of data on
energy and environmental policy, industry and market analysis,
managed to reject the perception that both government policy
and consumer attitudes in several key markets were changing in
favor of green technology. They insisted instead on the status quo,
so much so that over half of the new model lines were large size,
gas-guzzling SUVs and trucks, and the few business cases for
advanced technology vehicles were summarily rejected without so
much as a second thought. Needless to say, sales of the large size
vehicles continue to drop. Now, "hindsight is 20-20", and few of us
are able to consistently perceive subtle shifts in advance of the
time the changes become mainstream. But it is safe to say that in
many cases we could have sensed changes earlier than we did–if
we had been open to perceiving them. The tenacity with which we
hold onto our views, despite new and conflicting information, is
almost awe-inspiring. The executives in automotive I mentioned,
for example, to this day (in 2007) continue to suggest that the
moves of their competitors into green vehicles are folly, overly
expensive experiments with temporary technology solutions that
will only erode their profits. They may be right; yet most other

manufacturers seem willing to take the chance. The point is, the choices we make should be informed by a deep perception of all the forces at play, and not limited to data that supports our current positions.

Shared perception is also critical in complex systems where multiple stakeholders are needed to effect real, sustainable change. Most of us, being human, tend to see from the perspective of our own, narrow contexts. We either don't see each other across our institutional boundaries, or reject the perceptions of those who are at odds with our own. The challenge is to learn to see from the whole, to open ourselves to diverse and even conflicting perceptions. The arts-based approaches described a little later on are extremely useful in helping diverse groups open to and hold a shared perception rich enough to hold all the messiness of diverse perspectives and even persisting conflict.

Perception is the result of a discovery process, whereby we open ourselves to the complex layers of a situation by using all of our senses. Where many leadership development methods focus on observation and listening skills to deepen perception, before these can be expected to truly transform perception, we must first free our bodies to perceive. Indeed, the truth is in the body—the whole body, not just the head. The problem is that the body naturally limits sensory inputs to weed out the information that the brain deems essential—information that has been used by repeated habits takes precedence in our minds, so we can easily recall it when needed. When we need to do something new, however, our brains continue to operate based on old habits, limiting what might be needed to adjust behaviors and form new habits. The body is the vehicle through which we perceive, so it is essential to re-tune it as an instrument that can take in as much sensory information as possible. This is how we deepen perception.

Actors are trained from the beginning to learn how to open the body, using all of their senses, to fully perceive many diverse, often seemingly conflicting inputs from the situations (improvs) in which they engage. Boal describes the process of freeing our bod-

ies to perceive as "de-mechanization":

QUOTE

Augusto Boal

"*Every human activity, from the very simplest—walking, for instance—is an extremely complicated operation, which is possible only because the senses are capable of selection; even though they pick up all sensations, they present them to the consciousness according to a definite hierarchy, and this filtering process is repeated over and over in our daily lives....This process of selection and structuration results in mechanization because when confronted with similar circumstances the senses always select in the same way....For this reason, we must start with 'de-mechanization,' the retuning (or detuning) of the actor [a person who takes action]...He must relearn to perceive emotions and sensations he has lost the habit of recognizing.*"

Many people use contemplative practices such as meditation and yoga to connect to their physical and spiritual interiors; yet we tend to perform and seek benefit from these practices most often in our personal lives, outside of work. The point here is that, if perception is critical to our work, then maybe we need to use those contemplative, "de-mechanization" practices to also support our work, to tune our own instruments to perceive.

De-mechanization exercises used by actors work extremely well in freeing our bodies to perceive. (And, they are a lot easier to do than many other contemplative practices.) They take very little time (5 minutes or so), and can have profound affects. It might seem silly to dedicate time to these little exercises; I'd encourage you to try one or two, and see what happens inside of

you. (It is particularly helpful to use one of these exercises in conjunction with the more robust and complex methods suggested later in this section.)

What follows are a couple of easy de-mechanization exercises you can do anywhere, along with some stories from my experiences in using them.

Physical Meditation

The simple act of connecting with the physical interior of the self can allow surprising things to happen, in you, and in the way you later relate to others. Physical meditation helps to connect to the often hidden or forgotten "truth" that is in the body, stored away and unused. It can help break the body's habits of perceiving only selective information and to see anew.

It may sound crazy, but I did a physical meditation exercise (the one described below) with a group of senior executives, mostly engineers and manufacturing leaders from a company with a very traditional, formal culture. At the end of the exercise, one of the participants, a fellow I had known for a few years, suddenly got up from his chair, and motioned me to follow him out of the room. His shirt was soaking wet, and he was shaking. I thought he was ill. He then explained that something strange but wonderful had happened to him during the exercise. At first, he said, his mind was resisting, telling him it was stupid to be doing such a thing in a training session. But then, he explained, his body just "took over", and he suddenly felt this profound shift within him, an experience he hadn't had since he was a young boy.

I followed the exercise with a personal vision activity, after which my friend and several others told me that their visions suddenly became crystal clear, as if they had been there all along and simply re-emerged, now with a power and passion they had for

some time lost. It was quite beautiful.

I often tell groups that if they can trust in the simple work of re-connecting to the interior of the self, then vision work is easy—it just "pops", appears, without any effort at all.

EXERCISE

Directions for Physical Meditation

Before you leap out of bed when the alarm clock rings, or bolt from your chair to your next meeting, take just a few minutes to ground and "open" yourself by de-mechanizing your body.

- Sit or lie flat in a comfortable position, arms and hands resting comfortably.
- Close your eyes, and keep them closed throughout the exercise.
- Take a few deep breaths, in through your nose, out through your mouth.
- Imagine a little ball of light, a warm ball of energy. Visualize this little ball in the toes of your left foot. Move the ball over the front of your toes, then around to the back.
- Move the ball across the bottom of your left foot, and then over the top of your foot, then up to your ankle. Move it around your ankle.
- Move the ball up through the center of your calf, very slowly. Feel its warmth inside of your leg.
- Move the ball over your knee cap, then around the back side of your knee.
- Slowly move the ball through the center of your thigh, into your buttocks, and up into your lower back. Move it across your lower back, feeling its warmth.
- Move the ball slowly up your spine, into your left shoulder, all around your shoulder blade.
- Let the ball float down your left arm, into your hand, then through your thumb and each finger in turn.
- Slide the ball slowly up through the inside of your left arm, back into your shoulder, and into your neck.
- Move the ball around the base of the back side of your head, then across your scalp, back of head, top of head, then onto your forehead.
- Let the ball fall down over your face, first your left eye,

then right eye, over your nose, then mouth, across your left jaw, then right, then down into your neck again. Breathe deeply, and let the muscles in your face, jaw, neck relax.

- Slide the ball down into your right shoulder, and then all the way down your right arm into your hand, then into your fingers.
- Slide the ball slowly up through the center of your right arm, into your shoulder, then let it fall slowly back down through your spine, into your lower back.
- Feel the warmth of the ball in your lower back, breathing deeply.
- Slide the ball down through your buttocks, into your right thigh, then slowly down through the center of your right thigh into your knee.
- Move the ball over your right knee cap, to the back of the knee, then slowly down through the center of your right calf and into your ankle.
- Move the ball around your right ankle, feeling its warmth.
- Let the ball drop into your right heel, then slide under your foot, and into your toes.
- Let the ball drop out of your toes, breathing deeply.
- Slowly open your eyes.
- Slowly sit up and then stand.
- Try to hold the relaxed but present sense of your body as you move through the day.

NOTE: *For this exercise, it is important to be in a quiet place, and to keep your eyes closed, to keep your attention on the interior of the body, and not the exteriors that your eyes and ears perceive. It often helps to have someone talk you through each step, as outlined above. The same exercise can be done with groups.*

Walking Conscious

Most of us could literally walk in our sleep; we move through the world unconsciously. Watch a toddler walking, and it's easy to imagine the attention paid to each muscle, each movement. But most of us adults forget, and lose the conscious connection with our bodies. When this happens, our senses perceive less than they might. A friend, with whom I have shared ideas about many of the concepts and methods in this book, recently told me she had started to consciously pay

Grace getting ready to take her first walk on the beach.

attention to her body's patterns of movement and ways of sensing, and was shocked to discover how much she had lost touch with her natural ability to perceive. After spending just a little time consciously noticing, paying attention to her body's movement and ways of sensing, she said that she suddenly saw her colleagues as if for the first time, and noticed that her own quality of listening—of being "present" with them—was transformed. (She did, however, confess that holding that state is very hard to do!)

Work like this is hard for many of us—any working parent knows how hard it is to slow down! And, for those of us most comfortable operating from our heads, it feels very odd to be paying attention to our bodies. We believe that we ought to be doing more "important" things like thinking grand thoughts or doing something useful. Perhaps it's that comfort with the mind that allows our brains to talk us out of the simpler, perhaps truer

connections to our selves and each other.

EXERCISE

Directions for Walking Conscious

As another way of de-mechanizing the body, try to walk consciously, to open your body to perceiving both the self and your surroundings more fully.

- Sit comfortably in a chair.
- Hold a book or some other small object in one hand.
- Close your eyes and keep your attention focused on the interior of your body.
- Stand as slowly as possible, taking time to both feel and visualize each muscle that is moving your body upward.
- In slow motion, take one step forward, visualizing in your mind's eye each muscle, joint, and tendon that is moving you forward—thigh, knee, calf, ankle, foot, toes.
- Again in slow motion, take another step forward, this time noticing the muscles, joints, and tendons in the opposite leg.
- Drop the object you are holding; listen for where it falls, and sense if and where your body moves toward the fallen object.
- Slowly kneel to pick up the object, trying to sense it with your hands and body, without opening your eyes. Notice and visualize each muscle in your body as you move.
- Pick up the object, then stand slowly, visualizing each moving part of your body as before.
- Take another step, and another, trying to move a little more quickly while still visualizing the parts of your body as they move.
- As you move through the day, try to continue noticing your body's patterns of movement and ways of sensing.

Working in Slow-Reverse

We have patterns of habit, daily rituals and routines that we repeat over and over. These patterns are based on what we think

is most important, according to the sequence and time and quality of attention we dedicate to each. Some of the patterns are probably useful and necessary; but performing routines unconsciously over long periods of time causes us to block out that which doesn't fit a sequence or allotment of time. Those of us who are always too busy often adopt patterns that get us through the day as efficiently as possible, minimizing time with colleagues, family, and friends. While we all know that face time is important (and often pleasant), we often end up relying on the more convenient communication methods such as email, and in the process sacrifice what may be the most valuable sources of meaning and collective consciousness—***each other***.

RESEARCH

The Village

An innovative program developed in one of the more troubled public school environments in Los Angeles, The Village, has demonstrated that the simple shift of providing more personal attention to students can make the difference between success and failure in school. The program, developed for African American students who statistically perform at far lower levels than other ethnic groups in the same district, provides staff and time in family-like settings at the school, during the school day, to share everything from feelings about race and cultural identity to students' poetry. In just two years since the program's inception, the students' scores on the Academic Performance Index jumped 95 points, well above the district average—same classes, same teachers, same students, but huge improvements due to the simple shift in attention.

EXERCISE

Directions for Working in Slow-Reverse

Try disrupting your patterns of habit by doing the opposite of what you usually do, and spending time on the people and things you often neglect. Try also disrupting patterns of habit in your work group, to allow all of you to open to new perceptions and new ways of being.

- Rather than beginning your day by checking email (or whatever it is that you do when arriving in your office), pick up the phone or, better yet, drop by a colleague's office to check in with them, see how they're doing, what they're concerned about these days, what they are wishing for…
- Rather than skipping lunch and holing up in your office to get through your work, invite some colleagues to take a walk in the woods or a park.
- Rather than jumping into a meeting by tackling the agenda, slow down and start with a "check-in".
- Rather than meeting around a table, sit in a circle of chairs. Or, rather than using flip charts or PowerPoint, use crayons and large sheets of paper placed on a table, to draw together.
- Rather than leading a meeting (if that's what you usually do), ask someone else to lead it that day.
- Rather than…You can fill in the rest!

Bubbling Up

Many of us are trained from early childhood that emotion is inferior to intellect, and that we should control our emotions to avoid letting them cloud our judgment. Emotions are part of us, whether we acknowledge them or not, and, despite our brains' attempts to block them, they do affect us—what we perceive, what we want, what we fear, what we dream. When denied or

buried, emotions still have a huge influence on our actions. Because we have not acknowledged them, we often don't understand what we or others are doing! Groups who fail to deal with the emotional realities tend to get stuck, talking around and around issues, never quite getting to the heart of the matter. Some of the ensemble methods explored later on help with that challenge; but first, the individual needs to be able to connect to his or her own emotional truth.

When tapped, emotions can both ground and energize us. (Managers who wish for higher degrees of "motivation" and "passion" among employees could take the cue here, as those characteristics come from the heart, not the head, and from the inside, not from external incentives!) In situations where the challenges are extremely complex, even overwhelming, it is often the emotional energy that sustains us.

ACTING CLASS

Playing the Action, Not the Emotion

Actors spend a great deal of their training and rehearsal time in tuning their instruments—their bodies—so as to be able to easily access emotion. However, as most good acting teachers will caution, one does not 'play' emotion; one can only play an action. For example, if I am playing a woman whose daughter has suddenly awakened from a coma, I would not try to 'play' joy, but rather, as the script might dictate, go to her hospital room to talk to her; in seeing her and hearing her speak to me, joy will emerge if I have allowed myself to be open to it? Why.

Emotion happens, arises organically from within us; action is determined, based on will (which may be affected by emotion, but is governed, in the end, by choice). We do not need to force emotion, but rather allow it to surface, through our action, and in ways

that shape the quality and energy of our action. In this way action is rich, combining heart, head, and hand.

Work in the field of "emotional intelligence" has dispelled the head-versus-heart myths, yet breaking the habit of thinking over feeling is hard to do. The de-mechanization process focuses on freeing our selves to connect to and channel our emotions, so our actions can be both thoughtful and inspired.

EXERCISE

Directions for Bubbling Up

- Sit or stand in a comfortable, relaxed position.
- Close your eyes.
- Squeeze your eyes shut tight, then relaxed, 9 times in succession.
- Flex your nostrils, out, then relaxed, 9 times in succession.
- Purse your lips, sucking in at your cheeks (like a fish mouth), then move your lips apart, together, 9 times in succession.
- Breathe deeply from the pit of your stomach, in through the nose, out through the mouth. Feel the air and the energy in it moving through you as you breathe.
- Place your attention deep in the bottom of your stomach as you breathe; try to visualize the stomach and then the lungs expanding and contracting with each breath.
- Keep your focus on your breathing, and, after a little while, you will begin to notice emotions "bubbling up." Notice them, and allow them to fill you.
- Repeat the exercise over time to the point where, by simply connecting to your breath, you can allow emotional clarity to arise within you.

Situation: Observation and Perception Methods— Connecting to Collective Interiors

PRINCIPLE	COMPETENCIES & BEHAVIORS
Situation	**Pure Observation** • Observes fully using all senses, without characterizing • Places full attention on the subject of observation or interaction **Shared Perception** • Sees the situation inside of the organization or group in context of all stakeholders and conditions in the whole system • Describes own perceptions of context, events, and relationships from first-person perspective (emotional, relational, spiritual, physical manifestations) • Solicits perceptions from all key stakeholders in the system • Engages stakeholders in dialog to surface shared and differing perceptions • Crystallizes collective perceptions to move the "real work" to the center of attention • Holds both shared perceptions and persisting conflicts • Actively helps to maintain a holding space for the "real work" to be done

The de-mechanization methods free us to perceive, opening our selves to seeing and sensing the situation more deeply. In order to perform as an ensemble, however, we need to have a shared perception of the situation, the context both inside our institutions and the larger environment in which we operate. While there are countless methods for analyzing the exteriors of situations, we need to also give space for connecting to our collective interiors, the emotional, spiritual, and relational aspects of the situation, and to our selves as actors within it. Thus, shifting the quality of thought and action throughout a whole system requires us to essentially redefine the problem—not as something "out there"

to be changed or fixed, but rather something "in here", within each of us, and among us. This shift requires us to move from focusing on solo to ensemble performance, from "I" to "we," so together we can surface and operate from the deep source of our shared, collective interior.

I've used the word *"ensemble"* many times now—what's different about an ensemble than a regular team or group? Ensemble performance (ensemble being the adverb that characterizes the nature of group performance) requires a special type of interaction among the members of the group.

THESAURUS

Ensemble (adverb)

all together
as one
as a whole

Groups gather all the time, but don't necessarily perform "as a whole", and while sports teams often display ensemble interaction, workplace teams often fail to do so! The improvisation methods described previously outline what it is about groups who do perform well "all together" through ensemble performance. However, working as an ensemble is hard for us to do, especially in multi-stakeholder systems, across boundaries. The de-mechanization methods explained in the previous section help tune one's own instrument, preparing the self to interact more fully and more effectively with others, as part of an ensemble. (When de-mechanization methods are used with the same people who comprise the ensemble the shift into ensemble work is much easier— if one or two players in a jazz band aren't prepared to improvise along with the others, then the overall performance suffers.) The methods included in this section can be used to help diverse

groups (especially those in conflict or who are stuck), to first "sense" the situation as individuals, and then weave together their many diverse perceptions into a shared story of the reality.

No-man's Land

In order to effect change, we need to allow ourselves to be changed. For change in any of us to occur, we need to be open to surprise, open to discovering something new or unexpected. Otto Scharmer characterizes this movement within the self as "letting go" so as to "let come." For most of us, "letting go" is the hard part! What else have we got to hold onto but the old, familiar self with all its cumulative knowing? Wouldn't it be easier (and more productive) to simply further develop what the self knows and what the self can do? Much of our schooling and adult education is built upon the premise that attention to development of the self leads to better performance, in work and in life. It's interesting to me that actors tend to approach "performance" in quite the opposite way—by focusing on the Other. While actors do spend a great deal of time training their own instruments, by the time they get on stage with each other the focus shifts to the other actors and the shared situation in which they are all engaged. Actors accept the fact that they need to work as an ensemble in order to perform a play or do an improv, so attention to the Other is essential. (The same can be said of work in any context; our structures and processes only create the illusion that we can get work done without performing as an ensemble!) Theatre improvisation requires actors to develop ensemble skills because they have nothing (no script) but each other to rely upon in advancing their "play". It would be impossible to perform in an improv without maintaining deep attention to others in the ensemble, unless of course you were playing a crazy person! The same is true in work and life—

there is no script, and we have only each other to work with to make things happen. When we get stuck, especially in multi-stakeholder systems, it can often be the result of denying the fact of ensemble or failing to give the attention needed to the others in the system. If we need to work together to effect systemic change, attention to the Other is critical.

Because theatre (like life) is a group art form, whether script-ed or improvised, the role an actor plays is only revealed through his or her interaction with others. Interaction of this type requires intimate exploration of the other players, and allowing oneself to be surprised, to truly discover. One cannot afford to assume any-thing about the other characters or what might or might not occur as an improv unfolds. Discovery, in short, requires us to complete-ly forget the self and all of its biases, so we can fully attend to who or what we are exploring. Former Brandeis professor and theatre director Ted Kazanoff describes this process as "entering the no-man's land", a space where all attention shifts away from the self, completely letting go, and instead focuses on the Other, to discov-er fully another person or, in some cases, an external setting or event, and to trust that this discovery process will reveal not only the self, but the whole as a unified fabric, a collective interior. Now, entering the no-man's land is very hard for most people to do—our selves constantly want to interrupt and steal focus from the Other! Yet, when engaged in the discovery process of the Other, all of the senses are fully engaged, deepening perception and allowing for a quality of interaction that is otherwise nearly impossible. We shift from our selves as subjects (in Otto Scharmer's terms, from painters painting a painting) to observers of other subjects. It requires discipline, as well as a leap of faith. To begin developing the discipline, one must first cultivate deep observation skills.

Pure Observation

The way actors view observation is a bit different than what others in leadership development typically suggest. It is a subtle difference, but extremely important: the act of pure observation occurs without judgment, without characterizing or qualifying the subject. For example, if you were to observe your back yard or a park on a sunny afternoon, you might think to yourself, "The sun feels so good, and the sky is beautifully clear today." We unconsciously add attributes to what we observe. Likewise, in a meeting with stakeholders, some of whom you might have had frustrating experiences with in the past, you might observe to yourself, "Oh, she is always spouting her own point of view and never listens to anyone else!" When we characterize in this way, we keep ourselves stuck in the past, limiting what we can perceive and also what we allow others to *be* (at least in our perception of them). If we wish to transform a whole system, we must dispense with judgments based on past experiences, and simply observe *what is*, what is actually said or done, what is seen, heard, smelled, tasted, or touched (by the observer) *in the moment*. The truth only exists in the moment, so the ability to be fully present, with all the senses objectively attending to all the subjects present, is where surprise comes from. In the case of the meeting, one might, in each moment, simply observe: the woman from the city council is present, wearing a blue dress with short sleeves, her hair is worn up in a bun, and her eyes are bloodshot and her nose sunburned, and she is speaking very fast and very loudly, talking to her colleague, and arranging her notes in a stack. Now, you might ask, what good is all that information to you, someone at the meeting who needs the city council to approve your project (for example)? It is not the information, necessarily, that is of value; it is the act of the disciplined attention that allows us to notice things we sometimes overlook. We understand more deeply and allow ourselves to be surprised. We suddenly *hear* things that the hypothetical woman from the city council is saying that maybe we didn't hear before.

And, in many cases, the act of such focus allows us to notice things in ourselves that we usually do not allow into our consciousness. This trust in the moment, in placing our full attention on the Other, transforms us. And, to anyone who might be noticing, this attention can shift the energy and quality of interaction in the entire group—people can feel it when we are truly present with them. Try it, and see what happens. To begin, use the following exercise to develop the discipline.

EXERCISE

Directions for Pure Observation

- Take a pad of paper and a pen or pencil to a place which is very familiar—the cafeteria at work, a park, a restaurant, a community center or other busy place you know well. Be sure to pick a place that has lots of people in it.
- Find a place to sit. Observe the minute details of everything you see, hear, feel, taste, or smell one object, setting, or person at a time. Try to perceive as many precise details as possible (e.g., his hair is brown—no, it is light brown with strands of blond and some grey at the temples...) Be sure to use all of your senses to take in the information. Focus on the pure sensory facts of what you observe, taking care to avoid characterizing (e.g., no adjectives that describe how you feel about what you sense).
- After you finish observing each person, setting, or thing, write or draw exactly what you perceived, from memory, as objectively as possible. Notice if/when you tend to want to characterize what you perceived, then rewrite or re-draw your description.
- When you finish writing or drawing your description, compare it to the living example, noting how closely your description matches each detail of what you observed.
- Find as many opportunities as you can in everyday settings to practice observing details, objectively, and using all of your senses.
- Once you feel ready to observe fully, try the method when listening to others speak.

TRAVELOGUE

Sunset

Scene: A young family of four is walking west on a North-facing beach on Kauai, the older sister holding her little brother's hand as they pick their way over the lava flows that break in waves into the deep blue sea, Mom and Dad trudging through the drifts of soft sand heaved by winter swells ashore, now leaning in windward sloping mounds unbroken all the way to the rocky point that juts beneath Bali Hai, the East end of the Na Pali, the end of the beach, end of the road. It is a journey they make every night to watch the sun set.

The family stops at a crescent bay where a long sandy shoal stretches into the Pacific. An older couple is already sitting on the one long trunk of a driftwood tree. Another family of five is seated in the sand on the West-facing ridge that rims the bay, a black dog among them, also watching the sky as the sun begins to dip. A few clouds drift like slow-moving ships around the circumference of the horizon, gathering at the 'end' of the day in clusters around the sun, as if, too, to glimpse its descent. The wind blows from the leeward side of the island, soft but constant, carrying the smell of earth and green. Some ways down the coast, a couple hundred yards out to sea, the silhouette of a fisherman standing on the reef slowly moves toward the shore; he appears to be walking on water.

As the sun nears the rim of the sea, people scurry in two's and three's and five's from the tangle of palms and cypress that ring the beach, hurrying to take their seats along the shore to watch it sink from view. Mom and Dad grab the choice seats at the end of the point, leaving big sister and little brother to search for perfect pieces of coral and then to hurl them as far as possible

into the surf. The black dog saunters over to Mom and Dad and takes a seat with them, leaning on Mom to have his belly scratched.

Oranges, purples, pinks, and indigo blues seep up from the thin line where the water meets the sky.

Dad *(calling to the two children)*: There it goes…
Mom: Come watch…

(The children can be seen laughing, their voices drowned out by the shush-shush-shush of the surf.)

Dad *(calling more loudly this time)*: Grace and Max!
Max *(running up to the dog)*: Whose dog is this?
Mom: I dunno; he's a beach dog…
Dad *(patting the dog)*: He's a sweetheart.
Grace: Let's take him home.
Mom: We can't take him; he belongs to somebody…
Dad: Look—there it goes…
Max: You said he was a beach dog…
Mom: Look at the sunset…
Grace: The sun sets every day, Mom.
Max: He doesn't have a collar…
Mom: Watch until the sun sinks just below the edge of the water and sometimes you can see a green flash.
Max: Mom, how do you know he belongs to somebody.
Grace: Yeah, he's all dirty and skinny.
Dad: He's a beach dog, they get dirty…
Mom: Look, there it goes…Watch now…

(Pause, everybody watches for a second, then:)

Max: What if a tsunami came right now.
Grace: We'd run.
Mom: Look, it's almost down…

Max: How high is this over the water?

Dad: I dunno, about twenty feet.

Max: How big does a tsunami get?

Grace: Way bigger...

Mom: Wow, look at the colors...

Dad: Yeah, it's a good one tonight...There it goes...

Max: What if that ice shelf melts, then would there be any beach?

Grace: No, that's why they build the houses up on stilts.

Mom: Look—there! Did you see it? Did you see the green flash?

Dad: There's no green flash.

Mom: Yes, there is; you just can't blink, or you miss it.

(Everyone on the beach applauds, then get up to go home.)

Grace: Why are they clapping?

Mom: For the sun. In Key West, the whole town comes out every night to watch the sunset, and everybody claps. *(to Dad)* Remember that?

Max: Why?

Mom: Because it's beautiful.

Max: But the sun sets every day.

Mom: People need to remember how beautiful it is; if you don't pay attention, you forget.

(The dog rolls over on his back, and everybody pats him and rubs his belly.)

Max: How long will it take before the ice all melts?

Dad: Nobody knows...

Max: A long time?

Grace: No, not very long. And then there won't be any

beaches.
Max: Can we take the dog home?
Dad: No, he's a beach dog, he lives here.
Max: But where will he go when there isn't any beach?
Grace: He'll be dead before then.
Max: (*running down the beach, calling after the dog*)
Come on, boy! Come!

(*The dog runs after Max. Grace gets up and runs, too.
Grace, Max, and dog take a sharp right turn onto the
beach path that leads to the house, and then disappear
from view. Mom and Dad wait for the last bit of color
to fade from the sky.*)

Shared Reality

Just as there's not but one tree, not only a single fish, no stone
that is the same as another, there's no one reality. Reality is the
sum of everything, and of the whole of the countless perceptions
of all those who behold it. In work and life, however, we tend to
select those aspects of reality that we prefer or that most interest
us or seem to concern us; and in the process we leave out what
may be critical pieces of the picture which we all inhabit. To fully
understand a situation, in ways that allow diverse groups to collaborate (even when each member has a very different perception
about the nature of the situation), a sharing of realities is necessary. Otherwise, we are left with our own pictures and have no
common ground upon which to move together. As uncomfortable,
unpleasant, or overwhelming as a larger view of reality might be,
we cannot afford to risk ignoring the often messy and complex but
"whole truth" that creates the context for our action and interaction. The essential challenge in ensemble work is thus to first

allow oneself to perceive fully, and then to enter into the "no-man's land" to discover the many facets of reality as perceived by others, and then together to weave the many views into a larger whole, a shared reality.

In order to weave together the fabric of a shared reality, it is necessary to explore both the exterior manifestations of it as well as the multifaceted interior perceptions of the collective. Many of our leadership tools ignore the interior dimension, or segregate it from the more objective exteriors we tend to analyze to understand "current reality". And many of our methods and practices tend to lead us into dichotomies, conflicts that must be negotiated or differences to be reconciled, made to fit neatly and harmoniously into a mutually acceptable monochromatic plane. In the workplace, contradictions are often unwelcome rifts in the quest for certainty, and conflicts to be avoided and smoothed as quickly as possible — where we race to the movies or novels for drama (which is based on conflict), we avoid it at all costs in life! Yet conflict is the seed of creation, the source of discovery and self-surprise. If we do not let in new ideas, feelings, ways of being, especially those that most contradict our own perceptions, we discover little if anything at all. In the process of reconciling conflict and contradiction (which is simply the conflict of ideas or forces), we reduce ourselves to consensus, sacrificing things we care about or ignoring ideas, feelings, events, or people that do not neatly fit. And this is dangerous, because these things we have left out do not simply disappear; they linger, and sometimes seethe, inevitably to rear their ugly heads at some point down the road. True ensemble—a collective discovery and creation process—cannot exist when conflict is not allowed. The point is not to reduce complex and conflicting views, but to create a space that is large and rich enough to hold them all together.

Stories are one of the few forms that can be used to create holding spaces rich enough to allow deep exploration of exteriors and interiors, where contradictions and conflicts can co-exist in the same space. What's more, stories told by many voices can be

woven together in ways that slowly surface shared reality and eventually help the collective begin to move the real work to the center of our attention.

SIDEBAR

How Stories Help to Integrate Head, Hands, Heart

We often separate the act of thinking from feeling (what we want or what we don't want or fear) and from doing, which may end up an unintended mix of the former two dimensions of self, when they are not rectified. Stories capture events not only by recounting what happened, but also how the events affected the people in them. Stories describe roles of the characters within them not only by the tasks and actions they take, but also in terms of what they want, how they feel, and how they feel about each other. Stories can convey a point of view, a message, and also the nature of conflicting views, integrating what is thought with what is desired and what is done.

Similar to methods adapted from other art forms and wisdom traditions, the story-based approach allows individuals and collectives to:

- Make space for deep individual reflection through the heart—personal stories, not head-based analyses and detached observation.
- Connect to the deep source of our collective experience by structuring attention on the human, spiritual domain—what we feel and fear and love and dream, rather than focusing solely on the external

structures, roles, tasks, and results.

- Then, objectify or "suspend" the interior condition through these stories in ways that allow us to first see and acknowledge their emotional and spiritual essence, and, through this inner knowing, to better move from It to new ways of Being.
- Connect the self to the Other by "seeing" (to acknowledge or learn of) the stories of others in the system, from the place of their deep experience, in ways that allow us to feel those stories from the perspectives of the tellers (the same way any good story will move the reader into another reality).
- Structure our attention on the human dimensions of the interrelationships among the parts to reveal the whole—seeing the mix of connections, contradictions, tensions, and emerging aspirations of the whole system by linking and threading through the many voices to, finally, develop a shared story that captures the full complexity of the system.
- Move the shared story of current reality into a new, desired story of the future based on collective need and aspiration.

PLEA

Why One Story from the Many Voices

Many of us are well-practiced in systems thinking, yet the complexity of the systems in which we operate, along with severe limits on time and resources, make it very difficult to make space for continually seeing and engaging the whole system. Somehow, while we manage to make a small space for tuning our individual instruments, we tend to revert to playing within our compartmentalized songs—each to his own sector,

function, department, project, or team. Despite the best intentions, we tend to stop hearing the many voices, the many notes that comprise the whole of reality. We become deaf, and blind. We need to let come the song that lies at the core of our system, the one story or melody that captures the soul of our collective experience.

Story Weaving

Profound and sustainable change doesn't happen unless the voices of the many are brought to the center, and unless we integrate all dimensions of head, hand, and heart. Story Weaving is a method that helps to surface the many, diverse, and often conflicting perceptions of a situation, and to create a holding space that is strong enough to contain them in a shared view of reality, in all its complexity and messiness. The creative process of storytelling helps to break our ingrained habits. Using first-person narrative, metaphor, or pictures to tell stories, removes familiar modes of communicating and forces us to draw from a deeper source, to start from a "blank page". Describing experience from first-person perspective places us inside the system as human actors within it, and everything that entails. Learning to "presence" the whole system by virtue of the many first-person experiences allows us to relate to it in a very different way than analytical modes afford. Thus, Story Weaving is intended to give voice to the collective presence by providing a social technology for creating and sustaining:

- "Holding space" for the collective challenges, ideas, perceptions, and aspirations of diverse large-system groups (even when separated by points of view, geography, and time)
- Story-based approach to systems thinking (moving the "thinking" to "presencing") that enables the

gathering of the diverse "voices" of all stakeholders across the whole system to be heard and seen as parts of a shared whole

- Space for mirroring current realities of a system, and especially to those who are often left voice-less (the marginalized or unattended to, whether customers or disenfranchised groups who have been placed at risk under current systems)
- Platforms for surfacing shared pictures of the future that embody the physical, relational, and spiritual needs of the whole
- Focusing mechanisms to enable complex systems to place the real work at the center
- Means for leaders to develop future leaders by inviting voices at all levels of the system to participate in co-creation of new directions, new programs, new policy

MURAL

Story Weaving Structure

Individual Stories

Perceptions of the Collection of Stories

Shared Story:

Real Work

Use this structure to gather and weave together the stories from many 'voices' into a shared story, moving the 'real work' that emerges to the 'center'.

A simple, weaving structure (depicted on the previous page) is used to gather and *see* the diverse perceptions of the many in a larger view of reality, and then to surface key themes and conflicts that represent the real work at hand. A center *space* in the weaving construct allows for common themes and core issues to come to the literal and spiritual center, slowly building a shared story as a container for collective interiors, as one would weave a basket. Groups may then use the "story basket" as the springboard for live dialog (such as through circle or World Café[5] methods), systems mapping or other issue identification methods, and shared visioning sessions to co-create new realities.

DIRECTIONS

Story Weaving

Here are a string of methods to use in surfacing and weaving together stories of current reality, from the inside-out.

1 Select a "situation" that requires attention from many, diverse stakeholders.
2 Spend as much time as possible using the "observation" methods to observe as many facets of the situation as possible.
3 Write your own story about the situation, from your own first-person perspective of it, including the combination of the following (in any sequence):

- To describe this situation to a friend who knows nothing about it, from whom I would like advice, I would tell him or her...[e.g., topic, history, nature of problem/opportunity as I see it, who is involved and my relationship to them and feelings about them, recent events/actions that characterize the situation, what I want to do or wish I could do...]
- When I am most frustrated, angered, saddened, or dis-

illusioned by the situation, it is because I feel/think to myself…
- When I am most energized, driven, passionate about this situation, it is because I feel/think to myself…
- When I am alone and imagine this situation, it is like [pick a metaphor to describe or draw a picture that captures the essence of the situation, as I feel it]…
- When I think of the other 'characters' in this story (the other people involved, with whom I interact or who affect the situation in significant ways), I see them as…
- When I observe this situation, I see, hear, smell, taste, feel…[write observations without characterizing here, and note feelings that arise separately]
- What I hope will happen at the 'end' of this story is…
- What I think (or fear) will happen at the 'end' of this story is…
- I need…
- I want…
- I dream…

NOTE: *Do not worry about the quality of your writing; write as if you were speaking out loud to a trusted friend or loved one. If you have 'writers block', then tape record your story first, to transcribe it verbatim later. (Tape recordings can be used to share stories later, but it is a good idea to have written transcriptions so as to allow reflection on details.) If it is easier to relate any of your perceptions and feelings through illustrations or pictures, include them as you like. The most important thing is to relate your story truthfully, and to have the courage to simply and deeply 'tell it like it is'—for you.*

4 Once you have finished your own story, put it away for a day or two, and then read it. Try reading it out loud, to yourself or to a trusted friend.

5 Consider all of the different "characters" in your story (the people and groups involved in the situation). Make a list of these people, adding any you might have left out in your story. Be sure to include those whose "voices" are not often included in your

work, as well as those whose "voices" you would rather not "hear"! Select at least 6 people to participate in the storytelling and weaving process, as described below. At first, limit group size to about 20 or 30, to keep group sessions manageable; you can expand to include more "voices" later.

6 Invite all of the people on your list to tell their own first-person stories, based on the same situation, and using the same method described above. If needed to ensure truthfulness, stories may be written anonymously, and gathered by an independent party.

7 Gather all of the stories. Distribute all of the stories to everyone who participated in writing them, as well as any other key stakeholders you wish to enlist. Ask everyone to read through all of the stories, and to make notes about:

- What surprised me most…
- What I learned that I didn't know or acknowledge before…
- What moved me most…(for better or worse!)
- What is similar to my own story…
- What is very different from my own story…
- What seems most important among all of the stories (common themes)…
- Things I want to know more about…

8 Schedule a gathering of everyone involved, preferably in a place that is both neutral (when people in conflict or power positions are involved) and "away" from the situation you are exploring. Ask everyone to bring their notes (from Step 7 above), and to be prepared to share them in the group.

9 Ask an independent person to facilitate the gathering (someone with no vested interest in the situation, and with no position of power over others, who has good group dialog facilitation skills). During the

gathering, use the stories and notes from all the readers to "weave" a shared story, as follows:

- Ask everyone to share their notes from the stories; capture main points and perceptions on a large mural, leaving a big space at the center to begin to note common themes, deep conflicts, and areas of interest (whether solutions to these exist or not, and whether there is agreement about how to deal with them or not).
- Use Café dialog or other group methods (see "One Story", below) to explore the stories and perceptions of the "whole" of them. As collective perceptions emerge, note these in the center of the mural. Take care to hold also conflicting perceptions; do not lose them or let them go.
- Keep your mural in a central place, where people can review it over time, in between gatherings. (Take photos to distribute when people are separated geographically.

10 Based on outcomes from the gathering, schedule follow-up gatherings as needed to continue to weave your "story basket" until a clear sense of the real work is moved to the center of your collective attention. Capture this collective story in writing and pictures, so you can use it to "hold" your collective attention on what matters most as you move forward.

11 Use the collective story, including persisting conflicts, as criteria for your priorities and actions moving forward (e.g., subsequent sessions such as described in the next sections of this book, or as suggested through other methods, such as those for creating shared vision, systems thinking, strategy development, etc.)

12 Allow your story to evolve over time by gathering

stories from new people, revising your own stories, and/or evolving your collective story together.

Web-based approach

Where other methods adapted from the performing arts such as theatre and dance-based approaches rely on groups being physically present, the story-based approach can also addresses the challenge of geography and time constraints by providing a virtual platform for collective reflection and discovery, when large numbers of people need to be involved. As many institutions lack the monetary and human resources needed to conduct comprehensive stakeholder interviews, learning journeys, deep dives, or other methods used to surface diverse perspectives and deepen perception, this virtual form can produce the same results by leveraging new technology and our oldest form of making collective meaning, story.

If you have the resources, you can use a web-based structure to publish all of the stories and the outcomes of the "weaving" sessions, so many people in remote places can access them. You can also allow new stories to be added over time, so as to create an evolving, living story of your collective experience, mirroring your transformation. For information about how to structure a web-based Story Weaving forum, see the "Invitation" section at the end of this book.

Uses of Story Weaving

There are many practical and worthwhile uses for creating a shared story of our collective interiors:

- When whole system change is needed (e.g., generating a breakthrough in the quality of education for students at risk, in which grassroots organizations, education system, elected officials, and local business are needed to effect change)
- When complex subsystems wish to enact significant and sustainable change (e.g., creation of a comprehensive "health zone" in a local district to better address the HIV/AIDS crisis)
- For deep conflict resolution, in which stakeholders at odds can find ways to open to and hear the voices across the system, and co-create visions for alternative futures (e.g., gang crisis, in which gang leaders, law enforcement, and community members must somehow find a way forward together)
- For getting groups unstuck by surfacing and enacting creative tension from head, heart, and hand levels (e.g., a group of global executives who wish to restore quality of life and meaning for all employees throughout the enterprise)
- As an education tool for teachers to use in classrooms to inspire students to relate complex topics to their own aspirations and interests (e.g., science class learns about ecosystems through local environmental projects, weaving stories of all stakeholders in the system, and linking these to "first person" experiences of ecological concerns and aspirations for change)

One Story, Many Voices and Movements

The notion of getting to one story as told by many voices may sound simple; yet, it seems one of the central challenges of our

time. Amid the seemingly ever-widening and deepening conflicts among nation states, ethnic and religious groups, and just plain old little people who can't seem to figure out how to work together even when they share the same challenges, being able to get to a shared story through all the differing views and experiences of reality might be one of the toughest but most critical first steps. The difficulty in creating a shared story is not always due to conflict. Sometimes we cannot see the Other's experiences because we are too caught up in our own, and it can take a while to work through our own mishigas before we can let anybody else in.

A few years ago, while working with a school system, I joined a multi-stakeholder group of administrators, teachers, parents, and the occasional school board member, a special task force charged with strategic planning for the district. Our charter was to ensure equity and equality of education for all students, regardless of ethnic, economic, or other factors affecting both student and teacher success. Everyone agreed the vision for "equity and equality" was critical for the community, and well worth pursuing. It seemed a perfect starting point for the work. But in months of weekly meetings, the stories of the representative stakeholders created not clarity and unity, but a cacophony of desperate and disparate voices whose frustrations were so great that they couldn't hear one another. One night it was the African American parents who were insisting that advanced courses were excluding children of color. The next meeting it was a group of parents proclaiming that it was the gifted children who were being unfairly "left behind". Another night, the leader of a teaching team broke down in tears, professing she and her colleagues, having a workday from seven in the morning to eight or nine at night, could not work any harder or longer, and that there was little that could be done for any of the students beyond simply getting by, as they were. The next meeting was consumed by the administrator, supposedly leading the task force, who after two hours of minute detail describing the many wonderful programs the school had implemented, said she really didn't understand why we were

going through this strategic planning process anyway. And so it went, with story after story never finding the other storytellers, never letting anyone else in. We did, in the end, manage to come up with a reasonably good strategic plan. But, the experience left many members of the community disenfranchised, some even bitter. It was not what it could have been in forming a loosely structured but vital network that had within them the collective experience and even the aspiration to do something great.

I imagine that most of us have encountered similar situations in many different contexts. Everybody has a story, a true and important story. The tragedy is that we often forget to share our stories in ways that invite support, or lend a piece of a picture that may be connected to the other pieces, around which we might all work together to address shared challenges. How do we let each voice rise to be heard, and also find the other voices, through their own stories, in a way that helps us find each other?

I have encountered this dynamic enough now to believe that, first, it is necessary to let individuals and groups who are stuck simply express the extent of that "stuckness". Given time and structured space for both individual and group reflection, people can find their way from being isolated victims to becoming a community of true leaders. It's no good to simply vent, each person sharing his or her own laments in an endless series of complaints. It is, however, often necessary for individuals and groups to get their feelings and frustrations out, and this process has to run its course before they can move to generating solutions. When groups avoid dealing with their individual experiences of reality and jump too quickly to trying to create a shared sense of their collective experience, the result is often a watered-down version of the truth, one that has little meaning for anyone. Likewise, when groups in conflict try to jump to solutions without first dealing with the sources of their conflict, the solutions rarely stick. I have been exploring which types of structured spaces seem to best help individuals surface and connect their interior experiences to the larger story of their community. Both the Story Weaving and

One Story methods begin with the surfacing of individual stories, then use different structures to create a shared story that reflects the whole in ways true to all of the parts. It's a hard process to manage, but it can be very productive, even transformational, in the end.

DIRECTIONS

One Story, Many Voices and Movements

As a way to structure group synthesis of stories and perceptions of them (in the Story Weaving process, for example), and/or to allow collective experience to shape and evolve shared stories over time, here is an activity that can help one story to emerge from many voices, drawing from the interior of the mind, the body, the heart.

1 Select a situation to explore (or, use the situation and stories generated through Story Weaving).
2 Invite 6 to 20 or so people to a gathering to explore the situation. Ask an experienced facilitator to lead the gathering (taking care that this person has no vested interest in the situation and no power or authority over others in the gathering).
3 Start with a group de-mechanization exercise.
4 Then, sit or stand in a circle. Based on the situation/stories, allow each person in the circle to describe first verbally, then with a physical gesture or pose, each of the following, in turn:

  • One word or object that describes what I most sense as the nature or essence of the situation…
    • A gesture or pose that illustrates this essence…
  • When I see myself in the situation, I feel like a…
  • When I see us all together in the situation, it is like a…
  • I need…

- I want/desire…
- I fear…
- I dream…
- I will…
- (other…as you like)

NOTE: *Have everyone in the circle contribute to each topic above before moving to the next in the list. Have the facilitator record key words and themes on a mural (adding to the Story Weaving mural, if done previously). Consider using a graphic recording to draw what is expressed both verbally and physically.*

5 Give the group some time to reflect on what the facilitator has captured during the rounds. Then, ask them to find partners, and to take a dialog walk to reflect together on the collective "story" that appears to be emerging.

6 Gather as a group to share perceptions of the emerging story, capturing it on the mural.

7 Use the following ensemble methods to evolve and build on the story, and to move the system forward in co-creating new stories.

NOTE: *Unlike Story Weaving, the "One Story, Many Voices and Movements" method incorporates the use of physical gesture and pose, in addition to words, as a means of expressing individual perceptions. There's a good reason to include physical movement in addition to words: we can be very clever with words, using them to say what we think is correct or wants to be heard; yet when being forced to express our perceptions and feelings through a movement, gesture, or pose, most people will reveal their true interior. Because the use of movement is uncomfortable for many people, using it intentionally as a form of group communication places everyone in a vulnerable, almost intimate state.*

EXAMPLE

Truth in Movement

I experienced the power of movement as a group communication form in a very striking way when I participated in a "legislative theatre" session based on the methods of social activist and theatre director, Augusto Boal. The intent of these sessions is to bring together groups in deep conflict, and to use a series of theatre and improv-based techniques to help them first mirror their differing perceptions, and then co-evolve solutions. In this case, ideas actually end up as bills (the seeds for government legislation). The focus of this particular session was around a dispute over "gang injunctions," where known or suspected gang members were being served with injunctions that limited their freedom (such as curfews, house arrests, and other restrictions on where they could and could not go in the community). Attending the session were citizens from the community who were in favor of the injunctions, former and current gang members who opposed them, a fellow from Amnesty International, and a few other NGOs dedicated to finding solutions to gang-related issues. The non-gang affiliated citizens were convinced that the injunctions, while not always "just" (many having been served to people who had not ever committed any crimes), were absolutely necessary in order to maintain a safe community. The former gang members and NGOs were protesting the practice on the grounds it was a violation of human rights. I was amazed that these people had found their way to the same room, let alone to try to work out a solution together.

After a very awkward group dialog session, mostly restrained but impatient and tired testimonies from the

various stakeholders, the same words having been spoken in many contexts many times before, the leader of the session put us into a circle, standing facing each other. Each person had to take a turn making a physical "pose" or gesture—without using words—that represented how he or she was perceived by the Other. A few of the former gang members went first, and, much to my surprise, struck up angry, violent, and threatening poses depicting how they saw the non-gang people in the community seeing them. The people being portrayed were at first shocked, but then they began to laugh. They recognized themselves in those poses, and started talking about how funny it was, thinking it would be the gang members, not the "ordinary" people like housewives and school teachers, who would be seen as such frightening and threatening beings! When the non-gang members of the community had to take their turns depicting the gang members, the best they could do was mimic cliché styles of "gangster" walking and "ghetto" hand gestures used for greetings. The gang members thought this was really funny, and began instructing their fellow citizens in the proper use of hand signals, what nod to use when saying hello, and the difference between a nod to a friend and someone you don't know. In that moment, the relational "space" was totally transformed. Without any instruction from the facilitator, people just naturally sat down in small groups and started talking together, trying to figure it out.

Intention and Will Methods:
Connecting the Source to the Situation

PRINCIPLES	COMPETENCIES & BEHAVIORS

Will

Shared Will
- Surfaces individual will based on the common situation and the "real work"
- Surfaces and holds counter-will
- Engages others in synthesizing individual wills to crystallize shared will
- Holds conflicting wills of others with shared will for change

Role

Role Creation and Evolution
- Defines own role in context of the situation, the other roles involved, and the shared will to do the "real work" at hand
- Explores own role through interaction with others
- Evolves own role in ways that consistently demonstrate individual and shared will
- Refines own role to support other roles in effecting the common situation
- Adjusts role as needed based on changes in the situation or other roles

Once everyone has a shared story of the situation—including the many different and often conflicting perceptions of it—the challenge becomes connecting to the situation as both individuals and an ensemble, in ways that draw from the deep source of intention and will. Again, intention is what one *wants*; will is what one is determined to *do*. Both, together, give us the energy and drive to do amazing things. Shared intention and will based on a shared perception of the situation gives the collective the determination to do amazing things together, as an ensemble. When leaders and groups become stuck, or fail to enact the type of change they had hoped for, it is often because they have not clarified their intentions, or have not rectified intention with will, to the point of *choice*, particularly when the choices are hard. The gap between intention and will is often referred to as "counterwill", the fears, doubts, self-imposed obstacles, or other things that keep us from enacting our intentions. While these obstacles may always be present, the idea is to acknowledge the counter-will while at the same time making conscious, explicit choices that express our will through action, in light of or despite of the obstacles.

Shared Will and Role Creation

When multiple stakeholders are needed to affect a situation, it is especially important to generate *shared* will. While any one individual might take very different specific actions to enact will, depending on role, shared will is the shared determination to enact the change the collective seeks to generate. Shared will, based on a shared view of a common situation, enables large groups of people to perform well as an ensemble, where many individuals playing different roles can act in harmony, drawing from a collective source of commitment. However, getting to shared will can be very difficult, as it requires each of us to put ourselves on the line, to be willing to actually *do* something. It is at

this stage where things like vision (when not done well) can fall apart—what sounds good but is hard to do, or requires us to fundamentally change what we do, often doesn't get done, despite our good intentions! For example, if the situation is a troubled school district, in which Latino students are performing at far lower levels than other ethnic groups, and I am an administrator and you are a teacher, we might each easily come to the same intention: we want to improve the performance of Latino schoolchildren. However, when it comes to will—as expressed through action—either one or both of us might not be willing to make the kinds of changes needed to improve their performance, such as the things that could require a lot of extra work, for example, or time and money. While we might also disagree on the specific actions to take (e.g., new teaching methods versus special programming to supplement classroom work), if we don't get to shared will first, it is unlikely we will come to agreement about the specifics.

By spending just a little time and reflection on intention and will, leaders are able to more easily surface individual and collective aspiration, and in ways that lead to clarity in the choices they are willing—and not willing—to make. Once this clarity is achieved, specific actions become obvious, almost intuitive. Likewise, by defining roles based on shared will, pre-existing structural or relational boundaries are diminished, creating a shared space where each "player" can enact his or her own role, at last, as part of the same "play"!

DIRECTIONS

Wall of Will

Here is an easy exercise to use to clarify intention and will, first individually, then as a collective. (Note that this exercise often works best when preceded by Story Weaving or similar methods to allow groups to develop shared perceptions of the situation.)

When doing this exercise in groups, have one person play the role of facilitator, leading the others through the exercise. Conduct the exercise in a place where people have room to spread out, either in chairs in a circle, or to lie on the floor. Have one piece of heavy paper and one marker for each person participating, ready to distribute when noted.

1 Review the shared "story" of the situation (as evolved through Story Weaving or other methods that you have used to deepen perceptions of current realities).

2 De-mechanization Warm-up:
- Lie on the floor with your eyes closed.
- Visualize each part of your body, beginning with the toes on your left foot... Foot... Ankle... Calf... Knee... Thigh... (and so on).
- As you visualize each part of your body, try to move it, in isolation from the rest of your body.
- When instructed, continue to the next exercise, staying in the same position, eyes closed.

3 Will Meditation:
- Visualize the situation that you have described through your shared "story".
- Try to see yourself inside this situation. What is your role (the general part you play in affecting the situation)?
- Based on your role in the situation, and your own and shared perceptions of it, ask yourself: What do I want? (i.e., What is my intention?)
  - Based on this intention, ask yourself: Do I want this to the extent that my choices and actions will be based on carrying out this intention? (i.e., What is my will?)
- Visualize yourself enacting your will. Try to see what you are doing. Or, visualize images that are metaphors

that characterize the expression of this will.
- Locate the source of this will in your body; try to feel it.

4 Draw Your Will:
- Keep your eyes closed.
- You will be given a piece of heavy paper and a marker.
- With your eyes closed, draw a picture of yourself taking an action that best describes your will.
- Do NOT open your eyes.

5 Counter-Will Meditation:
- Based on your will, ask yourself: What else do I want that might either present obstacles to pursuing this will, or conflict with it? (i.e., What is my counter-will?)
- Reflect on your counter-will. Visualize the actions you might take to express this counter-will. Focus on those actions that might present the biggest obstacles to enacting your will.
- Locate the source of this counter-will in your body; try to feel it.

6 Draw Your Counter-Will:
- Keep your eyes closed.
- Turn your paper over to the opposite side.
- With your eyes closed, draw a picture that best describes your counter-will.
- When you are finished drawing your counter-will, try to release it, to let it go.
- Draw a line through this picture of your counter-will.
- Turn your paper back over to the first side, the picture of your will. Reflect on this will; try to feel it.
- Do NOT open your eyes; your pictures will now be collected.

7 Dialog Walk:
- When instructed, open your eyes, sit up slowly, and then stand up slowly.

- Look at the pictures. Can you find yours?
- Group One (one half of the group): Pick up your own picture. Then, select another picture from the floor that interests you.
- Take a walk with the person whose picture you selected (20 to 30 minutes).
- Share your will and any concerns about counter-will with your partner. Look for common themes and conflicting themes.

8 Shared Will Dialog Session:
- After returning from the dialog walk, tape all of the pictures of will on a large mural, around a big circle at the center. This is your "wall of wills".
- Sit in a semi-circle in front of the pictures.
- In turn, each choose one word that best characterizes your will.
- After everyone has had a turn, go around the circle again, this time trying to link and connect themes, using words that both represent your will and build on words used by others. (Have the facilitator capture these words in the circle on the mural paper.) Note words that stand out as being contrary or very different.
- Conduct a group dialog (or Café session, for large groups of more than 12), to try to crystallize a picture of an emerging shared will. Continue to notice and hold wills expressed by others that conflict with emerging themes. Inquire about each other's intentions to see if you can find common ground, or ways to see how the different wills can be enacted harmoniously within the common situation, and in ways that enable ensemble collaboration toward shared goals.
- Continue to meet to refine this will over time. (It can take some groups a while to get to shared will that is based on true commitment, not compromise!)

9 Role Creation and Evolution:

- Based on your functional and institutional or stake-holder role (e.g., as a teacher, or as a business owner, a policy maker for an NGO, etc.), reflect on it in light of the individual and shared will you have generated.
- Write a role description to outline both the tactical and relational aspects of your function in the system, that would 1) best allow you to enact the shared will to influence the situation 2) best "fit" with the other roles in the system to contribute to ensemble performance. As you write your description, keep the competency behaviors below in mind:
  - Defines own role in context of the situation, the other roles involved, and the shared will to do the "real work" at hand
  - Explores own role through interaction with others
  - Evolves own role in ways that consistently demonstrate individual and shared will
  - Refines role to support other roles in effecting the common situation
  - Adjusts role as needed based on changes in the situation or other roles
- Meet in small, cross-institutional groups to share your role descriptions. Coach each other to refine roles to make for a balanced and complete "cast" of characters needed to perform the shared "play". (Draw them out on a large sheet of paper, if needed, to help you see them all together more easily, and to identify any missing pieces.)
- Consider and discuss events or potential changes in the situation that might require any one of you to adjust, expand, or change your role.
- Be prepared to continue to evolve roles through the remaining ensemble methods.

Ensemble Performance Methods: Putting the Shared Story on Its Feet

PRINCIPLE	COMPETENCIES & BEHAVIORS

Ensemble

Action Observation and Adjustment
- Continually observes what is happening in the situation, across the whole system, at present (emotional, relational, spiritual, physical manifestations)
- Holds attention on the others in the situation, in each moment of interaction
- Adjusts own actions as needed to affect the present situation and/or to support others in affecting the situation, so as to enact shared will

Imagination
- Imagines what might happen next or in the distant future, based on past events, present events and interactions, and multiple possible outcomes
- Experiments with different choices and actions to continuously explore the present moment and alternatives for effecting change, individually and collectively
- Holds sources of pain and fear, with sources of joy and hope, in embrace of deep discovery
- Instills wonder

While a relatively small core of storytellers can be engaged in crafting the initial stories that start the Story Weaving process of generating a shared story of the situation, it may be useful or necessary to extend the audience and participants to a much larger group to effect systemic change. Theatre-based improvisation methods can be very useful in this case, as a small core group of performers can engage large audiences in both reflecting on and evolving the story. Theatre-based methods also physicalize experience, putting our stories on their feet in ways that help us perceive and participate in the emergence of a collective story much differently than purely written or verbal methods. Additionally, use of these methods helps to develop ensemble skills.

Interactive Theatre

Theatre, like other communal art forms, is one of the ways we
mirror current realities, holding them up for both individual and
collective reflection in ways that allow us to perceive the many
complex and often contradictory dimensions of our experience.
While today's theatre often places the audience in a passive or
silently reflective mode, early forms of theatre were highly interactive and participatory, with little boundary between audience
and actors. (Even in Shakespeare's day, audiences attending performances at the Globe were reported to be lively, loud, boister-
ous co-participators, calling out to actors and each other throughout the shows.) Some forms of contemporary theatre have
returned to the communal roots of the art form, inviting audiences to participate with actors as the comedy or drama unfolds,
or to change the story's outcomes. While many of the modern participatory productions are frivolous in nature, social activist and
theatre director Augusto Boal has devised a series of methods and
theatrical forms designed to remove the barrier between "actor"
and "spectator". Boal invites audiences to become "spect-actors",
free to engage in changing the scenes in the play as a way to both
mirror and evolve reality when groups are in deep conflict. (See
Boal's books, *Theatre of the Oppressed*, *Legislative Theatre*, and
Games for Actors and Non-actors for his wonderful methods and
approaches.)

Because theatre allows us to physicalize the essence of our
experience, from the perspectives of many different "actors", it
can be a useful tool for mirroring complex realities in ways that
both hold conflict and evolve resolution. While some people use
professional theatre troupes to develop political plays designed to
engage the audience in dialog about social or political issues, the
methods can be adapted for use by non-actors as part of a collective inquiry, conflict resolution or innovation process. For example, such methods have been used by schoolchildren in both
urban and rural areas in developing economies to reflect back to

the community their often unspoken ills, such as familial abuse and other social patterns contributing to self-perpetuating poverty, and by groups as diverse as law enforcement, recovering addicts, and convicts, to reflect and address the socio-economic causes of crime. The theatrical veil of production tends to allow voices that have been marginalized to speak what must be spoken to those who may not want to hear it (in the relatively safe space of the audience). As an interactive improvisation, engaging the audience in the scenes, the form provides a vehicle for rapid prototyping—playing out of alternatives in rapid cycles of experimentation, with immediate feedback from all stakeholders, in the audience and on stage.

For groups who wish to develop ensemble skills, the use of interactive improv provides rigorous practice in the essential skills of action-observation. Each player must continuously and deeply observe the others, in the context of an unpredictable and rapidly changing situation, and then adapt his or her own actions to advance the shared play. For those brave enough to try it, the experience can be both exhilarating and revealing—it is a great way to learn about ourselves, and each other.

DIRECTIONS

Interactive Theatre Improv

What follows is a method for using theatre improvisation with groups to mirror collective stories (such as generated through Story Weaving), and invite a wider circle of people to participate in the mirroring and evolution of the shared story. Note that this method must be lead by someone with theatre improvisation experience. What follows is a general description of a suggested process, to refine and embellish as needed.

NOTE: *Keep in mind that the purpose of this activity is to mirror and co-evolve our shared story of reality, not to stage the ultimate theatrical production or do the best "acting." Acting skill does not matter. What matters is honesty, and courage; with these anyone can participate. Also note that use of the activity also develops ensemble skills, shifting our story in ways that cause us to draw from our collective experience, no matter how painful or conflict-ridden it might be.*

1 Select a situation to explore (or, use the situation and stories generated through Story Weaving). Provide all participants with a short written description of the situation; include topic, setting, time, place, historical context, people involved, nature of their relationships, recent events, and nature of conflict or obstacles to be explored.

2 Identify the principle "characters" in the situation, focusing on those who most affect it, cause it, and are in conflict over it. Limit characters to 2 to 10. Write a brief role description for each character, focusing on what they do, what they have done, general attitudes, perceptions, and behaviors or characteristics.

3 Identify an event that best characterizes the situation and the nature of the conflict among the characters. (Note that conflict need not mean disagreement, necessarily, but can simply be something that presents an obstacle to getting what one or more characters wants, as described below.)

4 Invite key people who represent the characters or those related to them (by virtue of their roles and the situation), to attend an improv gathering.

5 At the gathering, assign people (actors or non-actors) to play each role identified. Have each actor explore her/his role, in light of the situation and event, by defining the following:
   - What do I want out of this situation (intention)?
   - What am I willing to do (will)?

- What am I am afraid to do, or what else do I want that might be opposed to expression of my will (counter-will)?

6 Assign remaining people in the group to the role of observer, to later engage as they wish during the improvisation (as described below).

7 Based on the situation and event, set up an improvisation that includes 2 or more of the characters at one time. Allow the actors to play out a scene, based on the situation and their own intentions and wills.

8 When the scene ends (or begins to flounder or seems to get "stuck"), stop the action. Invite volunteers from the audience to replace any one or more of the actors, and to either replay or continue the scene, offering their own perspectives, intentions and wills.

9 Repeat the process, allowing replacements, as needed.

Summary of Methods

The methods included in this section of the book can do much, in my experience, to develop shared aspiration and capacity for change, particularly in cases where multi-stakeholder groups must collaborate across boundaries to make a profound and sustainable difference. The methods can be used independently, or in combination with one another. It doesn't take much time—a few hours to a few days, or short periods over time, depending on how deep you want to go. However, because cultivation of all of the ensemble improvisation competencies is required to fully tune the self and the collective, I suggest trying at least one of the methods for each competency. I have developed a "pathway" that strings together several of the methods in a sequence that can be added to with related approaches (such as

systems mapping and appreciative inquiry). To obtain detailed descriptions of the pathway, along with the purposes and outcomes of each of the methods suggested, please see the last section of this book.

Interlude

MUSICAL

Penmar Park (excerpt)

(Scene 1: The park at night. Lights just coming on, one by one. Tinny recording of Für Elise plays from the ice cream truck, offstage. The kids begin to appear in ones and twos, the entire cast. Following poem-song is delivered by ensemble, one line per person or pair.)

Penmar Park

ENSEMBLE:
When the sun goes down
And the lights come on
In Penmar Park
When most other parks die
People here come out
Like stars in the night
There's the ice cream man
Plays Für Elise
Mariscos truck
Hot tamales
And old Joe's van
Homeless guy
But he don't bother nobody

And no one knows why
But kids here still play in the sandbox
Still swing on swings
Play hustle on the half-court

And Friday night games
Same teams since we were old enough to dribble

For some reason gangs don't come here
Cops don't even pass by
Like nobody knows that we're here
Like the lights are a force field
A fortress protected by sidewalks
And the few square blocks
Under Mrs. Rodriguez's watch
We got our own rules
('Cept lights out at eleven):
No fighting
No trouble
Everyone plays

Been this way since we can remember
Never knew why

Act Two:
One Square Mile —
Building the Future We Want,
One Block at a Time

The methods suggested in the previous section of this book are intended to help individuals and collectives work from the inside-out, to surface and tap into the generative force of our interiors to enable us to achieve together what we have been unable to accomplish alone. While these methods do well to focus on the interiors of our experience, they are all rooted in current reality, in *what is*—useful, but limiting. It might be useful as well to look at the potential in starting totally fresh, from a true contextual blank page or empty stage, to explore unencumbered *what might be*, free of the constraints of current realities, interior and exterior! This is the extreme "empty stage" that groups are confronted with in crisis.

Such an approach might seem to require a degree of transformation (or, at least, creative destruction) that is unrealistic and undesirable. Yet it may afford the greatest creative potential, and, in situations where problems have persisted for a very long time, might be the only useful alternative left. At the least, starting fresh can be a very powerful way to get unstuck, to take ourselves out of the quagmire of messes, and truly *imagine*.

A NEW STORY

Eddie in the Next World

It is dusk in the city, and in the fast-descending darkness a vast expanse of high grass rocks sleepily in the summer heat, nodding to the shells of burned-out apartment complexes, barbed wire fences, and empty streets, once the scene of urban strife, now laid bare by men's defeat of themselves and each other, a wasteland where now only the wild grass can seem to grow. From the heavens above, this expanse of grass looms like a hole in the city, an empty space to fill...And even if only angels can dream of it, the weary and shattered, the lost and hungry among us too weak and dissolute to dream, in this void, this tiny patch of a single square mile, life could begin anew...This I tell myself, over and over, a prayer, a mantra, a plea. And I go to this place, this empty square mile, in my heart, in my head, in my soul, standing at what seem to be impassable gates, looking in at the nothing which is everything and could be anything, fearing and loathing the fact that I am still like a vagabond, wandering without direction, foolish and maybe even crazy, worse, like a beggar who can only look in from the outside, hoping someone else will come along to set things right (or at least lend me a few pennies of hope to fill my empty cup of a being that I am).

And I say to myself, "This is not enough."

I see this "empty stage" approach as a literal place, *"one square mile"* of an empty patch of land that could become the field for profound change, a microcosm of the larger wholes that would contain all the necessary things a community needs to sustain itself, invented from the ground up, without any preconceived notions about structures and forms, institutions and relationships. I believe humans have the capacity to build whatever we want, and to have the courage to start over when what we've done just doesn't work. What's more, I think we know enough about how the world works (and doesn't) that if we could start fresh, we might build in ways that deal with the whole system (all that is needed to govern and sustain, to learn and to heal), and not try to build each piece in isolation, hoping it will fit with the rest! So, this "one square mile" is, for me, both a metaphor of possibility and also a potential place to prototype and practice whole new systems that might stop producing messes (or at least the same sorts of messes our current systems fail to fix or perpetuate). It is a holding space for a systemic vision of profound and sustainable change, born from the inside of our individual and collective dreams, and built through our heads and hands in ways that are true to our hearts.

So, if we started fresh, unencumbered by the current messes, what kind of civilization would we build?

What would its citizens need and dream? What would the community that could fill those needs and allow those dreams to flourish be like? Any one community is a microcosm of society, indeed, the world. It holds the spaces for living and for learning, for working to sustain life and healing to make us well, and for celebrating and enjoying life together. Thus, the future of our planet lies within each neighborhood, and within each of us who inhabit both the present and the possibility. If we were free to build whatever future we wished, what would we create? What makes us think we are not free to do it?

Here is a picture of the starting place:

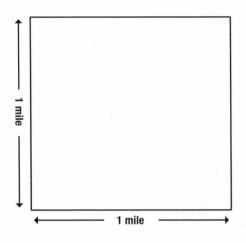

Building from the Inside-Out, Ground-Up

PRINCIPLE	COMPETENCIES & BEHAVIORS
Ensemble	**Imagination** • Imagines what might happen next or in the distant future, based on past events, present events and interactions, and multiple possible outcomes • Experiments with different choices and actions to continuously explore the present moment and alternatives for effecting change, individually and collectively • Holds sources of pain and fear, with sources of joy and hope, in embrace of deep discovery • Instills wonder

So, if we had this empty patch of a square mile (or even a kilometer or two), what would happen if we started by asking ourselves: Okay, what do we (all of us) need (to sustain ourselves)?

What do we want (really)? And what is our will (what we are determined to do to take care of our needs and wants)?

Maybe we could design such a system, with all the parts properly put together as an interdependent whole, and in ways that directly serve our needs, wants, and wills.

Here is a way to approach an empty square mile of a challenge, from a whole-system perspective, inside-out:

DIRECTIONS

One Square Mile

1 Gather a group of leaders from different parts of a community or global system (from government and non-governmental agencies, healthcare and education, business, etc.).

2 Agree to focus on an imaginary, metaphorical place, an empty space to fill in so as to sustain and nurture a whole community of citizens who might one day inhabit this space.

  • Agree that you each will draw from your own expertise, BUT without assuming that any of the existing institutions, practices, or policies exist (or will exist) in this new space. In fact, for the sake of instilling the discipline of imagination, don't let those existing exteriors into this new space, at least for the time being.

3 Draw a giant square on a big piece of mural paper. As a group, while reflecting on this empty space to fill in, ask yourselves:

  • Who will live here?
  • What will they need in order to sustain themselves and the physical environment in which they inhabit?
  • What might they want in order to feel safe, happy, at peace...whatever...?
  • What kinds of services and settings might best satisfy their needs and wants? (e.g., places and opportunities to learn together; places and opportunities to grow and

make and trade things needed to survive; shelters; places and occasions to get together...)

- Try to see "outside-the-boxes" of current structures and institutions. For example, learning can occur in many ways and places, not just in schools, as can healing and wellness, as can shelter, as can trade...

4 As you generate ideas, begin to draw the new community space in your empty square. Keep talking and drawing and re-drawing, continually checking yourselves against the criteria you generate for need and want (will comes later). If you are working in a large group, rotate to new tables (a la Café methods) to generate and build upon a wider and more diverse pool of ideas.

5 When you have had enough fun with imagining and creating this new community, compare it to current realities, from the perspective of your own piece of the system, and of the whole system. (If you have done a Story Weaving exercise, then compare the new vision with that picture of reality.) Ask yourselves:

- How does our new community serve needs better (or worse)?
- How does our new community serve wants better (or worse)?
- In what ways might all the different services and constructs and players in the new community work together differently (better or worse) than in our current system?
- What are the opportunities to test (prototype) new aspects of the system, the whole system, or new relationships (ways of working together across institutions)?

6 If you generate ideas that resonate deeply with the group, conduct the shared will exercise (from the previous section of this book) to surface what you are

collectively willing to do.

7 Discuss ways to quickly and easily prototype your ideas (simple models that can quickly be created with little time and cost, to revise and evolve easily). Be sure to prototype all aspects of the interdependent systems you have created; otherwise, the data gained by testing pieces of the simulation will likely be faulty.

8 If you do prototype new models, then test them against your original criteria for need, want, and what you later determined as will.

NOTE: *Lots of people do brainstorming and out-of-the-box types of visioning sessions. The important thing here is to engage and co-evolve the whole system, "The Everything" that is needed for any one piece, player, process, or institution to work—really work. And, to do this imagining in ways that focus on what really matters most, to people, all people.*

Epilogue

CONCERT

Day and Night

Some months after Eddie was shot, my daughter performed in the end-of-year choral concert. I was relieved to find the school campus unchanged, Barnum Hall looming steadfast on its bluff overlooking the Pacific, The Greek amphitheatre where Eddie's memorial service had been held cradled in silent darkness within the hillside just below, empty but waiting to be filled again by happier occasions, the pep rallies and assemblies, the graduation ceremony next week to celebrate those who had made it through and could go on to college.

The parents, friends, alumni filtered into the theatre, programs excitedly rustled through the evening's lineup—the school's music program is the pride of the community, known throughout the country and indeed the world for performances as good or better than many professional adult groups, performed by our students—a seemingly unlikely mix of rich and poor, an ethnic rainbow (almost more diverse by virtue of the fact that the kids include a mix of jocks and the more studious types, the popular and the shy), all equally surprised at what they found they were capable of creating, as well as celebrity typically relegated to school athletic heroes. People show up to see the concerts like going to a football game.

The program noted the night's theme: "Day and Night", an exploration of the "tidal forces" associated with light and darkness, as written by a number of

poets and in spiritual literature through the centuries, composed by the likes of Bach, Brahms, Monteverdi, Debussy, Claude Rene, to be sung in German and Latin, French and English, with one number performed in the syllables and sounds spoken by an Amazon tribe, the Krao, who speak in the sounds of the rainforest, for which there is no literal translation. Given what the school had been through that year, one race riot, two shootings, one death, and a host of invisible pains and crimes in between, it was a bold choice on the part of the musical director.

The concert was late in starting. At last, a group of boys shuffled onto the stage, wearing the uniform of a barbershop quartet. They sang a few early American classics a capella, apparently a curtain-warmer act. They were then replaced by a female chorus who performed a few jazz numbers. Parents new to the school's music department shuffled through their programs, trying to figure out who these performers were, and what they were doing—they hadn't been listed, and were certainly off-theme. Before another group, an all-male chorus that went by the name of The Testostertones, could take over the stage, the Dean of Students grabbed a microphone, her long grey hair flapping over her buoyant girth, and announced cheerily: "It looks like the student groups will be performing for us for awhile. As many of you know, these groups are self-organized, conducted, completely arranged by the students—we have nothing to do with it!" She beamed and turned the stage over to The Testostertones. The audience, most of whom were well-accustomed to the deference to the self-organizing student groups, applauded the apparent anarchy, cast down their programs, and settled into a masterfully sung version of "Under the Boardwalk."

And then, at last, the lights dimmed. The "official" program would now begin. The entire body of the school's seven collective choral groups entered the auditorium in silent streams, flowing like a soft but steady wind down the outside aisles, over the stage, and back again, completely encircling the audience. And then they began to sing, softly, somberly, beautifully, Eric Whitacre's "Sleep":

> *"If there are noises in the night,*
> *A frightening shadow, flickering light,*
> *Then I surrender unto sleep,*
> *Where clouds of dream give second sight.*
> *What dreams may come both dark and deep,*
> *Of flying wing and soaring leap,*
> *As I surrender unto sleep."*

Their voices emerged from the darkness, felt as much as heard, like a baby's fingers groping, tentative, gentle, curious, and intent, one section of the chorus at first reaching then receding, giving way to another, then another, and another, their singing wafting around the hall, curling like sweet smoke, rising and swirling, echoing from one side of the room to the other, joining then diverging, rising at last again to a single, final note, making the circle whole once again.

And I began to cry.

To this day, when I hear them and see them in my mind's eye, I cry, for joy, for sorrow, for the painful love of possibility.

The Way Forward

QUOTE

Gandhi

"Be the change you want to see in the world."

Menlo Lab

Since I started writing this little book, something wonderful has happened: leaders from big business and local government, school districts and healthcare, grassroots organizations and global NGOs, from throughout the US and many countries around the world, have been gathering around a shared dream to "clean up the messes" we have made, and to heal our societies, one community at a time. As an extension of the Presencing Institute, this dream is now emerging into reality as a deeply held intention on the part of these leaders, who believe in the core of their beings that they must (and will) work together across our many boundaries to generate meaningful social innovations that can begin to address the interdependent "crises" in poverty, education, healthcare, and all the related challenges pervading so many of our communities. It might seem surprising, even unbelievable, but the sheer number of these leaders, many from what might seem the most unlikely institutions, is swelling so fast it is truly extraordinary, and an undeniable sign that the world is changing, for the

better. Among the many wonderful places where leaders like these are now gathering, this network is what we call Menlo Lab. Inspired and named after Thomas Edison's famous Menlo Park Lab, where he and his team of inventors produced "the most concentrated outpouring of invention in history," the modern-day Menlo Lab seeks to invent the "social technologies" that support leaders in collaborating to initiate and sustain profound social innovation. In what is now a fast-growing, self-organizing network, the members of Menlo Lab are supporting several communities in extensive change intervention and capacity development projects, dedicating our selves and our institutions to the mission of generating well being—for all people.

While we see that so many of our communities continue to be plagued with a host of highly complex, systemic problems, "persisting crises" in our economic and social systems, we believe we have the innate ability to "be the changes we wish to see in the world". In fact, we believe that the human capacity to adapt and innovate in ways that can overcome even the most daunting challenges of our time is boundless. The potential in our collective wisdom and creativity, our natural tendency to generate well being, and the transformational power of our aspiration and will, present the opportunity to approach our challenges through a new type of social innovation that can unleash our human capacity to not only deal with the problems facing us today, but to create the future we want.

The Menlo Lab Approach

Innovation that allows us to tap into the full extent of human potential requires a fundamental shift in the way we approach our problems and ourselves as change agents within them. While there are, no doubt, a host of structural, regulatory, and econom-

ic obstacles to social innovation, these are the result of what we humans in the system have created. Research shows that failure to address these "exterior" obstacles is most often due to "interior" barriers within ourselves. Our approach is thus to focus on the self as the gateway to transformation, and through it, to transform our ways of being as a collective community of leaders who, together, can envision and enact social innovation.

Additionally, if we are to approach change systemically, to engage the many interdependent pieces of our whole community systems, we need to move from independent, institutional action, to cross-institutional *collaboration*. This requires us to cultivate both the relational and structural capacities to work together across boundaries to achieve shared aspirations. The challenge is that we are taught to work within our own individual institutional boundaries, so when the occasions for collaboration arise (most often in extreme crises), we struggle to collaborate. While the macro structures that so often divide us may not change much in the short term, we *can* develop the relational bonds and leadership practices that will allow us to transcend formal structures and, together, to forge generative approaches to whole system transformation.

Thus, our approach integrates the cultivation of social innovation capacities on three interdependent dimensions that shape our ways of being and our actions: the individual, the collective, and the systemic (structures and environments). By focusing on both the "source" of human potential and the "habitats" needed to nurture and sustain innovation, Menlo Lab intends to advance answers to the following questions:

- What conditions (personal, relational, and contextual) allow people to collaborate effectively across boundaries to generate social innovation?
- What individual and collective leadership capacities are required to create the right conditions?
- What types and means of support are needed to enable leaders to sustain change, over time?

Drawing from our network of practitioners and consultants, we are now engaging leaders at the local community level to explore their true needs and aspirations, to offer what methods and practices we have to serve those aspirations, and to collaborate in co-evolving new methods that may be needed over time. Please see the "Invitation" below for more about our work and how to join us in fulfilling the Menlo Lab intentions.

Invitation

Menlo Lab is a "circle without an edge", a community without boundaries, organized around shared intention and core beliefs about the approaches to personal and systemic transformation. We recognize that there are many other networks, learning communities, and individuals out there who share our intentions and beliefs, and hope we can share in both the learning and the work of "cleaning up the messes" by healing our selves and our societies so as to generate new ways of thinking and being that will lead to a better future. So, this book is intended to be an invitation to those of you who are doing whole system change work, in any sector (government, NGO, business), who would be willing to share your experiences so others can be inspired by and learn from them. While this book is fixed in print, stories will be gathered and shared using the Web, providing a virtual "holding space" for the people and communities who are doing this type of work, along with "living examples" others might learn from. People need to know about the many wondrous things happening out there, especially in these dark times. So please contribute what you can to this growing community by contacting me at:

tracyhuston@ca.rr.com

To learn more about Menlo Lab, please visit:

www.menlolab.org

And, please watch for evolving concepts, practices, and living examples related to the approaches explored in this book by visiting

www.solonline.org
www.collectivewisdominitiative.org
www.presencing.org

Additionally, if you would like to use any of the methods explored in this book, I have woven them together into an action research and change intervention process. This process, a "pathway" I call it, is intended to be used by the leaders of multiple institutions who inhabit a shared system, and who wish to together change that system, drawing from the source of their collective interior. For detailed descriptions and directions for how to use the pathway, help with using the pathways yourself, or if you would like to exchange ideas, practices, methods, or explore other related areas together, please feel free to contact me (email address above).

Acknowledgements

I would like to offer my deep thanks to all of those who inspired the ideas in this book, especially the members of Menlo Lab, Presencing Institute, and The Society for Organizational Learning, and also for the work of Otto Scharmer, Peter Senge, and Augusto Boal, and for the lives and futures of my children, Grace and Max.

References
and Sources

1 From the song "Heaven" by the Talking Heads

2 For detail on "presencing", see Otto Scharmer's book, *Theory U* (Society for Organizational Learning, 2007). See also the book, *Presence*, by Senge, Jaworski, Scharmer, and Flowers (2005)

3 For information about the Presencing Institute, see *www.presencing.org*

4 For information about the emerging field of "collective wisdom", see *www.collectivewisdominitiative.org*

5 For World Café dialog methods, see the book, *The World Café* by Juanita Brown and David Isaacs (2005) and their website at *www.theworldcafe.org*

About the Author

Tracy Huston works with leaders from business, education, healthcare, and local communities in developing the capacities and practices needed to enact systemic transformation. As a consultant and coach in support of large system change initiatives, her work focuses on the integration of personal, relational, and systemic conditions that enable both the individual and collective to achieve the results they want. She continues to collaborate with others in developing new social technologies needed to generate social innovation.

Tracy is the founder of the Menlo Lab, and an active member of the Presencing Institute and the Society for Organizational Learning.

p 17 - Shared song - transformation

p 19 - space - dance of nature   (EC)

pr 44 - 48   Leaders   (gas - system - R1
                         Brexpt   Throne

70 - 71   impров - creative
75 · 77   ☆ competence - shared!!

82   perceptions. (imgo to life of changes
                         now)

Whole system -   Cosmos
                  —————
                   Earth
                              R1

103   proven for "Story Wrong"